Objective Type Questions in Library and Information Science

{For UGC-NET, SLET, JRF & Other State Level Competitive Examinations}

Objective Type Questions in Library and Information Science

{For UGC-NET, SLET, JRF and Other State Level Competitive Examinations}

By

KANCHAN KAMILA

Ess Ess Publications

New Delhi

Objective Type Questions in Library and Information Science

{For UGC-NET, SLET, JRF & Other State Level Competitive Examinations}

ISBN: 978-81-7000-665-7

Rs.700/-

First Published 2012

Published by:
Ess Ess Publications
4831/24, Ansari Road,
Darya Ganj,
New Delhi-110 002.
INDIA
Phones: 23260807, 41563444
Fax: 41563334
E-mail: info@essessreference.com
www.essessreference.com

Cover Design by *Patch Creative Unit*

Printed and bound in India at Salasar Imaging Systems.

Dedicated To

My beloved younger daughter

"DRIPTA"

Who is no more

CONTENTS

PREFACE

This book is a product of extensive efforts of several years. It is based on "'All in One" approach because it will be helpful for NET/SET/SLET examinees, Library and Information Science (LIS) job oriented examinations and interviews, as well as for LIS students, scholars, and teachers. It contains three volumes.

It includes almost each and every modern concept of LIS. So, not only NET/SET/SLET questions and answers but also many more relevant questions and answers are available in this book.

Most of the examinees have been facing problems to answer the paper-III questions, hope, this problem will be solved in a certain extent. Because detail discussion of almost all new concepts will be helpful to answer the paper-III questions also.

It is impossible to include each and every concept of LIS syllabus but efforts have been made to make this book as exhaustive as possible, this book, which contains paper – II questions and answers from 1990-2010. It is hoped that this book shall be very useful for the aspirants for the new objective type pattern of Paper-III as per latest revision by UGC.

Questions and answers are arranged according to year wise NET questions arrangement not as per units as shown in the NET syllabus. I think the book will help a lot. Any comments and suggestions from reader community are most welcome.

— **Author**

ACKNOWLEDGEMENTS

I acknowledge Sri Soumitra Biswas, Assistant Librarian of University BT & Evening College, Cooch Behar (W.B.) for his mental support to me.

I am greatful to Sri Tuhin Sanyal, Asstt. Prof. (English) of Tufanganj Mahavidyalaya, Tufanganj, Cooch Behar (W.B.) for his valuable opinion regarding the choice of title of this book.

I indebted to Dr. Biswajit Das, Assistant Librarian of the University of Burdwan , Golapbag, Burdwan, for his constant inspiration to complete the book.

I am greatful to my colleague Sri Prafulla Kumar Pal, Assistant Librarian, Uttar Banga Krishi Viswavidyalaya for his great support.

I acknowledge Sri Janardan Roy, my former colleague and Assistant Librarian of the University of Burdwan, Golapbag, Burdwan and Ex-Prof. Swapnadip Thakur, Dept. of Chemistry, the University of Burdwan, Golapbag, Burdwan, my friend, philosopher and guide for their mental assistance.

I am fateful to my father Sri Kshudiram Kamila and my mother Smt. Sukhada Kamila for giving me such an attitude of "not to frustrate but to win". Without their immense contribution such voluminous work would not be completed.

I also acknowledge Sri Jayanta Kamila, father-in-law and his family for their positive support.

I am indebted to my elder brother Mr. Gautam Kamila, sisters and all other family members.

Last but not the least, my special thanks goes to my wife Smt. Sumita Kamila and my elder daughter Dipanwita Kamila to give me a space to work peacefully.

— Author

Paper II :
MULTIPLE CHOICE QUESTIONS AND ANSWERS

(From 1990-June 1998

Old Type Net Questions)

(All Answers in Bold Letters)

SUBJECTWISE ARRANGEMENT

SYSTEMATIC BIBLIOGRAPHY & REFERENCE SERVICE

1. Name of the President of the Royal society, can be found in
   (a) World of Learning
   (b) Commonwealth Universities Year Book
   (c) **International Who's Who**
   (d) Statesman's Year Book
2. Times Literary Supplement is most useful for
   (a) **book reviews**
   (b) news about Great Britain
   (c) digest of newspapers
   (d) library holding of U. K.
3. Information about Sahitya Academy Awards can be found in
   (a) World of Learning
   (b) Universities Handbook
   (c) **India: A Reference Annual**
   (d) Dictionary of National Biography
4. INB is published by
   (a) National Library, Kolkata
   (b) **Central Reference Library, Kolkata**
   (c) INSDOC, New Delhi
   (d) NASSDOC, New Delhi.
5. Library Herald is published from
   (a) Denmark (b) Paris
   (c) London (d) **Delhi**.
6. BBIP is a
   (a) National bibliography (b) **trade bibliography**

(c) universal bibliography (d) none of the above.

7. The coverage of Cumulative Book Index is
(a) **throughout the world**
(b) throughout USA
(c) throughout UK
(d) throughout India.

8. British National Bibliography is published
(a) fortnightly (b) monthly
(c) bi-monthly (d) **weekly**.

9. Periodicity of INB is
(a) annual (b) half yearly
(c) quarterly (d) **monthly**.

10. Books In Print covers
(a) **throughout the world**
(b) throughout India
(c) throughout Sri Lanka
(d) throughout China.

11. Person(s) attempted to compile a universal bibliography is/are
(a) H. E. Bliss
(b) C. A. Cutter
(c) S. R. Ranganathan
(d) **Paul Otlet and Henry La Fontain.**

12. Subject encyclopedias are designed to satisfy the need of the
(a) beginners (b) **subject specialists**
(c) all types of users (d) none of these.

13. The persons associated with user education activities are
(a) S. R. Ranganathan & G. Bhattacharyya
(b) F. W. Lancaster & Blaise Cronin
(c) **Louis Shores, Patricia B. Knapp & Thomas G. Kirk**
(d) none of these.

14. One of the aspects of reference service useful to the freshman is
    (a) user education (b) **initiation**
    (c) users behaviour study
    (d) users information needs study.
15. For the bibliographical details of Fiedel Castro you will consult
    (a) University Handbook
    (b) Encyclopaedia Britannica
    (c) Encyclopaedia Americana
    (d) **International Who's Who**.
16. The author of 'National Library of India: A Critical Study' is
    (a) **P. N. Kaul** (b) B. Guha
    (c) S. R. Ranganathan (d) S. Seetharama.
17. The author of 'Little Science Big Science' is
    (a) F. W. Lancaster (b) Blaise Cronin
    (c) Martia Bates (d) **Derek De Solla Price**.
18. 'India: A Reference Annual' is a
    (a) Handbook (b) **Yearbook**
    (c) Biography (d) Encyclopaedia.
19. The author of 'Penny Rate' is
    (a) M. P. Satija (b) A. N. A. Raju
    (c) Ramansu Lahiri (d) **W. A. Munford**.
20. The source of information for the quotation 'early to bed and early to rise, makes a man healthy, wealthy and wise' is
    (a) Handbook of Quotations
    (b) Encyclopaedia of Quotations
    (c) Yearbook of Quotations
    (d) **Dictionary of Quotations**.
21. Ulrich's International Periodicals Directory is a
    (a) primary source (b) secondary source
    (c) **tertiary source** (d) none of these.
22. User education was experimented for the first time by
    (a) **Monteith College** (b) SNDT College

(c) Trinity College (d) Presidency College.

23. The name of Vice Chancellor of Karachi University can be found in
(a) Encyclopaedia Britannica
(b) Encyclopaedia Americana
(c) International Who's Who
(d) **Commonwealth University Yearbook**.

24. 'Putting Knowledge to Work' was authored by
(a) Franz Kafka (b) Leo Tolstoy
(c) Charles Dickens (d) **Pauline Atherton**.

25. The Publisher of 'Who's Who of Indian Writers' is
(a) Ess Ess Publications (b) Orient Longman
(c) S. Chand Publication (d) **Sahitya Academy.**

26. The first Library Science journal of the world 'Library Journal' was published in
(a) 1877 (b) 1878
(c) 1879 (d) **1876**.

27. The 'New Encyclopaedia Britannica' is issued in
(a) 1 part (b) 2 parts
(c) **3 parts** (d) 4 parts.

28. A 'Bibliography of Bibliographies' is a
(a) primary sources (b) secondary sources
(c) **tertiary sources** (d) none of these.

29. 'Library and Information Science Abstract' is published by
(a) ALA (b) **LA**
(c) IFLA (d) ILA.

30. 'Referral Service' is
(a) the other name of Reference Service
(b) the other name of Indexing Service
(c) the other name of Abstracting Service
(d) **directing the user to another institution/individual where he can get the required information**.

31. 'World of Learning' falls under the category of

(a) Yearbook (b) Handbook
(c) **Directories** (d) Encyclopaedia.

32. The document in any library entitled 'The Hindu' is a
(a) General Dictionary (b) Dictionary of Quotations
(c) Thesaurus (d) **Yearbook**.

33. The editors of Encyclopaedia of Library and Information Science are
(a) Leonard Montague & Robert Pelczar
(b) Robert Stryer & Allan Hopkinson
(c) Michael Ferreira & Robert Cock
(d) **Allen Kent & Harrod Lancour**.

34. Recent arrangement of New Encyclopaedia Britannica is
(a) classified (b) **alphabetical**
(c) alphabetical classed (d) none of these.

35. The source of information on current periodical publication in India is
(a) Press Trust of India (b) News Trust of India
(c) **Press in India** (d) none of these.

36. Bibliography of International Scientific and Technical Dictionaries was published by
(a) UNISIST (b) **UNESCO**
(c) IFLA (d) FID.

37. World Bibliography of Bibliographies edited by Alice F. Toomey was published from
(a) Prentice Hall (b) Orient Longman
(c) Willey Eastern (d) **R. R. Bowker**.

38. Which of the following material would you not expect to find in a public library?
(a) Newspapers (b) Audio Cassettes
(c) **Patents** (d) Maps.

39. Which of the following is a union catalogue?
(a) Ulrich's International Periodical Directory
(b) New Serials Titles
(c) Press in India
(d) **NUCSSI**.

40. Which of the following is also available on CD-ROM?
    (a) INB
    (b) **Indian Science abstracts**
    (c) National Union Catalogue of Scientific Serials in India
    (d) Indian Books in Print.

41. Books in Print could be categorised as
    (a) National Bibliography from India
    (b) Trade Bibliography from India
    (c) National Bibliography from USA
    (d) **Trade Bibliography from USA**.

42. Which of the following is not a secondary source of information?
    (a) an encyclopaedia (b) a textbook
    (c) **a thesis** (d) a statistical digest.

43. Concordance means
    (a) **an alphabetical index to a book or author's work**
    (b) a multi lingual dictionary
    (c) an explanation of idioms
    (d) none of these.

44. Indian Library Science Abstract is published by
    (a) ILA (b) **IASLIC**
    (c) INSDOC (d) NASSDOC.

45. A "gazette" gives information about
    (a) places to see (b) history of places
    (c) old records and notifications.
    (d) **official announcements**

46. Referral service means referring users to
    (a) reference books
    (b) other books in the collection
    (c) **sources outside the library**
    (d) online search.

47. A special library has hand books, patents, research reports, manuals, technical digests. Which of the above are primary sources?

(a) manuals (b) technical digests
(c) handbooks
(d) **patents and research reports.**

48. The NUCSSI is published by
(a) National Library, Kolkata
(b) Central Reference Library
(c) **INSDOC** (d) Delhi Public Library.

49. To answer the question 'Recent articles on Ethnic Problems in Sri Lanka' we use
(a) Biological Abstracts
(b) **Sociological Abstracts**
(c) Mathematical Abstracts
(d) Chemical Abstracts.

50. India: A Reference Annual is an example of
(a) periodical publication (b) **serial publication**
(c) quarterly publication (d) foreign publication.

51. Her Majesty's Stationary Office (HMSO) is a publisher of
(a) **British Government** (b) American Government
(c) Russian Government (d) Indian Government.

52. Atlases form an important source of
(a) statistical information
(b) **geographical information**
(c) biographical information
(d) economic information.

53. Materials which are original in nature is known as
(a) secondary sources (b) **primary sources**
(c) tertiary sources (d) printed sources.

54. Sources consists of information that is distilled and collection of primary and secondary sources is called as
(a) Directory sources (b) Reference sources
(c) **Tertiary sources** (d) Bibliography sources.

55. Which database supplement the existing card catalogues and can be consulted for comprehensive searches?

(a) DIALOG (b) **OPAC**
(c) MEDLARS Database (d) OCLC.

56. A systematic summary of the knowledge that is most significant to mankind is known as
(a) **Encyclopaedia** (b) Directory
(c) Yearbook (d) Handbook.

57. A well-organised list of written, printed or otherwise produced record of civilization e.g. of books, articles in periodicals, etc. is called as
(a) Catalogue (b) **Bibliography**
(c) Union Catalogue (d) Indexing Periodical.

58. An interactive system, using telephone lines and is available to subscribers only is denoted as
(a) Teletext (b) **Videotext**
(c) Online access (d) Dialog.

59. Yearbooks and annuals are
(a) primary sources (b) ready reference sources
(c) **tertiary sources** (d) bibliographic sources.

60. Bibliography deals with the study and detailed description of documents is known as
(a) Enumerative bibliography
(b) Systematic bibliography
(c) **Analytical bibliography**
(d) Descriptive bibliography.

61. Who is referred to as the father of encyclopaedias?
(a) **Johann Henrich Alsted**
(b) Aristotle
(c) John Harris
(d) Seville.

62. 'Indian Books in Print' is an example of
(a) **trade bibliography** (b) national bibliography
(c) universal bibliography (d) subject bibliography.

63. 'Chemical Abstracts' is published
(a) fortnightly (b) yearly
(c) monthly (d) **weekly**.

64. The State-of the –art reports can be grouped into three categories a) reviews and survey b) advances and progresses and c)
(a) **trend reports**
(b) current awareness bulletins
(c) yearbooks
(d) research reports.

65. To present consolidated information available in various forms and to repackage the same in a condensed form for users is the main purpose of the
(a) Survey (b) Reviews
(c) **Trend Reports** (d) State-of the-Art Reports.

66. Reviews are of two types 1) subject oriented and 2)
(a) research oriented
(b) topical
(c) chronological
(d) **focusing in particular scientific or technical problem and its solution.**

67. Which reference source provides an account of the general direction of research in the subject based on a review of the documents on current developments?
(a) Current Contents (b) **Trend Reports**
(c) Reviews (d) Advances.

68. Glossary, Lexicon, Thesaurus, Vocabulary are some of the alternate names for
(a) bibliography (b) acronyms
(c) encyclopaedia (d) **dictionaries**.

69. Polygot refers to
(a) bilingual dictionaries
(b) **multi-lingual dictionaries**
(c) subject dictionaries
(d) language dictionaries.

70. The reference source often used for a stock of words and phrases with brief explanations and meanings restricted to a single work or author is known as
(a) Lexicon (b) Thesaurus

(c) **Vocabulary** (d) Glossary.

71. 'Encyclopaedia of Library and Information Science' is published by
(a) Bowker and Saur (b) **Dekker**
(c) Cambridge University Press
(d) McGraw Hill.

72. 'World Book Encyclopedia' is an example of
(a) general encyclopedia (b) subject encyclopedia
(c) universal encyclopedia (d) **children encyclopedia**.

73. The first edition of Encyclopedia Americana was published in
(a) **1920** (b) 1732
(c) 1829 (d) 1817.

74. 'University Handbook: India' is published by
(a) UGC (b) **AIU**
(c) Ministry of Human Resource Development
(d) University of Delhi.

75. The ready reference sources are complementary as well as supplementary sources of
(a) dictionaries (b) **encyclopaedias**
(c) bibliographies (d) patents.

76. 'Famous First Facts' is an example of
(a) **handbook** (b) encyclopaedia
(c) yearbook (d) directory.

77. Almanacs are grouped into three categories namely (a) Astronomical (b) Informational and (c)
(a) National (b) International
(c) Physical (d) **Topical**.

78. 'National Register of Social Scientists in India' is an example of
(a) statistical sources (b) almanac
(c) **directory** (d) yearbook.

79. 'BIS Handbook' is a catalogue of around
(a) 20000 Indian standards with alphabetical index
(b) **13000 Indian standards with alphabetical index**
(c) 2000 Indian standards with alphabetical index

(d) 1,70,000 Indian standards with alphabetical index.

80. The Patent Information System (PIS) of India was set up in 1980 at

(a) New Delhi (b) Pune
(c) **Nagpur** (d) Chennai.

81. The International Patent Documentation Centre (INPADOC) is situated in

(a) **Vienna** (b) UK
(c) Russia (d) Australia.

82. 'Standards World Over' is a publication of

(a) ASTM (b) BIS
(c) **ISO** (d) IEO.

83. 'Gazetteer of India: The Indian Union' is published in

(a) 3 volumes (b) **4 volumes**
(c) 2 volumes (d) 5 volumes.

84. 'Census Atlas National Volume' is an example of

(a) local atlas (b) historical atlas
(c) **demographic atlas** (d) anthropological atlas.

85. 'Current Geographical Publications' is published by

(a) Royal Geographic Society, London
(b) **American Geographical Society**
(c) The British Library
(d) Bowker – Saur.

86. 'International Who's Who' is published by

(a) **Europa** (b) Bowker – Saur
(c) Wilson (d) Marquis.

87. 'National Biographical Dictionary of India' is published by

(a) S.P.Sen (b) Durga Das
(c) **Jagadis S. Sharma** (d) Times of India.

88. 'Social Indicator of Development' is a publication by

(a) **World Bank** (b) UNESCO
(c) FAO (d) ILO.

89. 'World Tables' is a

(a) UNESCO publication

(b) **World Bank publication**
(c) UN publication
(d) IMF publication.

90. 'Asian Recorder' covers
(a) 40 countries (b) **45 countries**
(c) 50 countries (d) 55 countries.

91. 'Facts on File' is a
(a) current awareness service
(b) SDI service
(c) **loose leaf service**
(d) statistical service.

92. 'Data India' is published by
(a) **PTI** (b) Times of India
(c) INFA (d) Hari Sharan Chhabra.

93. 'Summary of World Broadcast' is published by
(a) **BBC** (b) Chadwyek-Healey
(c) Doordarshan (d) CBS Television.

94. To deal with enquiries for information that could be answered through non-documentary sources, is generally known as
(a) bibliography centre (b) information centre
(c) reference centre (d) **referral centre.**

95. Which institution was established to provide referral service globally, for all sources of environmental information?
(a) **UNEP** (b) UNESCO
(c) UNCTAD (d) UNICEF.

96. Which institutions are highly specialised types of information institutions that emerged to provide critical, analytical and evaluated support services to institutions involved in high level research?
(a) **IACs** (b) Libraries
(c) Documentation Centres (d) Referral Centres.

97. Which persons are engaged in activities such as translations, printing, publishing, publishing, etc.?
(a) Information gatherers

(b) Information processors
(c) **Information recorders**
(d) Information generators.

98. Forms of communications that involve creativity, persuasion and impact of the massage carried by them is known as
(a) Multimedia (b) Public relation
(c) Mass media (d) **Advertisement.**

99. Which is a pervasive part of modern culture, a medium to build up images of a society ?
(a) Mass media (b) Public relation
(c) **Advertisement** (d) Multimedia.

100. Among the print media that carry contents of mass communication which occupy the centre?
(a) **daily newspapers** (b) journals
(c) books (d) pamphlets.

101. Reference service is an example of
(a) anticipatory service
(b) current awareness service
(c) **on demand service**
(d) retrospective search service.

102. The information desk for the scientific and technological community which does not provide enquirers with the information they need, but suggests sources likely to satisfy their needs is known as
(a) Information Analysis Centre
(b) Documentation Centre
(c) **Referral Centre**
(d) Data Centre.

103. Modern information services which are considered as extension of reference service place emphasis on
(a) library oriented, need based reference service
(b) information oriented, need based reference service
(c) **user oriented, need based reference service**
(d) documentation oriented, need based reference service.

104. Bibliographies, indexes, abstracts and the like, answers the questions relating to
    (a) persons
    (b) places
    (c) meaning of words/phrases
    (d) **literature references.**

105. Organising and presenting the collected information in the form of a report acceptable to the user is one of the step of
    (a) ready reference service
    (b) short range reference service
    (c) **long range reference service**
    (d) anticipatory information service.

106. Which programmes are aimed at developing skills in users in literature search, consulting different types of tools and preparing their personal information files?
    (a) User studies (b) **User education**
    (c) Reference services (d) Information services.

CATALOGUING THEORY

1. 'Canons of Cataloguing' were first formulated by
    (a) Seymour Lubetzky (b) C. A. Cutter
    (c) **S. R. Ranganathan** (d) A. Panizzi.

2. According to CCC (Ed. 5) Ministry of Education, Government of West Bengal will be rendered a
    (a) West Bengal, Ministry of Education
    (b) West Bengal, Education (Ministry of ...)
    (c) **WEST BENGAL, EDUCATION (Ministry of...)**
    (d) Ministry of Education (West Bengal).

3. Which of the following is a pseudonymous name?
    (a) Suryakanta Tripathi 'Nirala'
    (b) George Orwell
    (c) **Prem Chand**
    (d) Mahadevi Verma.

4. ISBN consists of
   (a) 8 digits (b) 14 digits
   (c) 10 digits (d) 12 digits **<presently 13 digits>**
5. British Museum catalogue code was formulated by
   (a) S. Lubetzky (b) C. A. Cutter
   (c) **A. Panizzi** (d) C. C. Jewett.
6. Cataloguing in Publication stands for
   (a) co-operative cataloguing
   (b) **prenatal cataloguing**
   (c) selective cataloguing
   (d) descriptive cataloguing.
7. MARC was first launched by
   (a) The British Library, London
   (b) **Library of Congress**
   (c) INSDOC
   (d) DESIDOC.
8. OPAC stands for
   (a) **Online Public Access Catalogue**
   (b) Online Processing of Automated Catalogue
   (c) Online Programmers of Analogue Computer
   (d) Online Programmeming and Control.
9. 'Three cards system' is used for
   (a) cataloguing of books
   (b) **acquisition and control of periodicals**
   (c) shelf list
   (d) circulation of books.
10. 'Shelf list' in a library is used for
    (a) stock verification (b) **shelving of books**
    (c) acquisition of books (d) selection of books.
11. Canon of modulation is concerned with
    (a) canon of array (b) **canon of chain**
    (c) canon of ascertainibility
    (d) canon of recall value.
12. According to S. R. Ranganathan the two canons for chain are

(a) canon of ascertainibility and recall value
(b) canon of array and filiatory sequence
(c) **canon of decreasing extension and modulation**
(d) none of these.

13. Analytical entry is known in CCC as
(a) CRIE (b) **CRE**
(c) BIE (d) CIE.

14. The latest canon of cataloguing enunciated by S. R. Ranganathan is
(a) canon of ascertainability
(b) canon of modulation
(c) canon of decreasing extension
(d) **canon of recall value**.

15. ISBD was first introduced in
(a) AACRI, 1967 (b) **AACRII, 1978**
(c) AACRII-R, 1988 (d) AACRII-R, 1993.

16. Analytical entry is prepared for
(a) composite books (b) periodicals
(c) yearbooks (d) **part of a document**.

17. Rules for description are not given in
(a) ALA Code (b) Jewett's Code
(c) **AA Code** (d) AACR Code.

18. UAP has been sponsored by
(a) ILA (b) ALA
(c) LA (d) **IFLA**.

19. Rules for Dictionary Catalogue was devised by
(a) S. R. Ranganathan (b) S. Lubetzky
(c) **C. A. Cutter** (d) A. Panizzi.

20. Dr. S. R. Ranganathan undertook a comparative study of five cataloguing codes in the works of
(a) Definition of Cataloguing
(b) Objectives of Cataloguing
(c) Principles of Cataloguing
(d) **Headings and Canons**.

21. In AACRII, size of a document 20.5 cm. 32 cm can be written as

(a) 20 cm. 32 cm (b) 20.5 cm. 32 cm
(c) **21 cm. 32 cm** (d) none of these.

22. The concept of Principle Author recognises by
(a) AA Code (b) ALA Code
(c) British Museum Code (d) **AACRI & II Code**.

23. AA Code was devised by ALA & LA in the year of
(a) 1907 (b) **1908**
(c) 1909 (d) 1910.

24. Vatican code was published in
(a) 1930 (b) **1931**
(c) 1932 (d) 1933.

25. MARC was launched in the year of
(a) 1965 (b) **1966**
(c) 1967 (d) 1968.

26. ISBN is given in the main entry of
(a) AACRI (b) CCC
(c) **AACRII** (d) AACRII-R.

27. Title that does not disclose the subject of the work is called
(a) sub-title (b) parallel title
(c) **fanciful title** (d) none of these.

28. The latest edition of classified catalogue code is
(a) 2nd (b) 3rd
(c) 4th (d) **5th**.

29. The particular canon of cataloguing prescribes that the information found on title and overflow pages should be used for preparing main entry is
(a) canon of parsimony
(b) canon of recall value
(c) **canon of ascertanibility**
(d) none of these.

30. The main reason for using uniform titles as headings for certain works in a library catalogue is
(a) because users generally look under the particular title

(b) because users generally look under the single title
(c) **because users generally look under the uniform title**
(d) none of these.

31. According to CCC the best way to make the choice of heading is to depend on the
(a) canon of symmetry
(b) canon of individualisation
(c) **canon of ascertainibility**
(d) none of these.

32. Concept of 'Prenatal Cataloguing' was first developed by
(a) C. A. Cutter (b) **S. R. Ranganathan**
(c) S. Lubetzky (d) none of these.

33. The purpose of a 'see also' reference in a library catalogue is to direct a user from a
(a) standard term to the non standard term
(b) semi standard term to the standard term
(c) semi standard term to the non standard term
(d) **non standard term to the standard term.**

34. A book with two or more independent contributions is called
(a) simple book (b) complex book
(c) compound book (d) **composite book.**

35. In CCC, if the name of the author is taken from outside it will be put within
(a) **square brackets** (b) round brackets
(c) second brackets (d) none of these.

36. The code based on ICCP is
(a) CCC (b) AACRII
(c) AACRII-R (d) **AACRI.**

37. The institution not associated with the preparation AACRI was
(a) ALA (b) LC
(c) LA (d) **ILA.**

38. According to AACRII when the title page gives the name of only editor, the main entry will be made
(a) **under the title of the book**
(b) under the editor of the book
(c) under the compiler of the book
(d) under the translator of the book.

39. 'Cataloguing in Publication' programme was introduced by
(a) ALA (b) **LC**
(c) LA (d) British Library.

40. ICCP was held in Paris in the year
(a) 1960 (b) **1961**
(c) 1962 (d) 1963.

41. The code does not allow to find out information from outside the title and overflow pages in determining the choice of heading
(a) British Museum code
(b) Jewett's code
(c) Cutter's Dictionary Catalogue code
(d) **Vatican code**.

42. According to AACRII when there are four authors and no one is principal author and one editor, the entry will be prepared under the
(a) author (b) editor
(c) **title** (d) subject.

43. To carry out a search on 'Poverty in Gujrat and Rajasthan' a search statement would need to be framed as
(a) **Poverty AND (Gujrat AND Rajasthan)**
(b) Poverty AND (Gujrat OR Rajasthan)
(c) Poverty OR (Gujrat AND Rajasthan)
(d) Poverty OR (Gujrat OR Rajasthan).

44. According to AACRII, if a book has been edited by four persons, the main entry should be under
(a) the first editor (b) all editors
(c) **title** (d) the first three editors.

45. A list of books and other reading materials available in a particular library is called as
(a) Union Catalogue (b) **Library Catalogue**
(c) Bibliography (d) Dictionary Catalogue.

46. A list of date wise record of reading and reference materials acquired by a library is denoted as
(a) Shelf List (b) **Accession Register**
(c) Catalogue (d) Bibliography.

47. If a catalogue represents the collection of two or more libraries, it is known as
(a) Accession List (b) Bibliography
(c) **Union Catalogue** (d) Trade Catalogue.

48. The first edition of Ranganathan's classified catalogue code appeared in
(a) 1930 (b) **1934**
(c) 1964 (d) 1945.

49. The book 'Rules for a Dictionary Catalogue' was written by
(a) Ranganathan (b) **Charles Ammie Cutter**
(c) James Duff Brown (d) R. A. Cutter.

50. Sheaf form of library catalogue is also referred to as
(a) card (b) ledger
(c) printed (d) **loose-leaf**.

51. Which consists of strips mounted on a frame or cards held flat, hinged and with edge of each card protruding so as to make the heading visible?
(a) Microform card (b) Three card system
(c) Catalogue (d) **Visible index card**.

52. The microform catalogues are being used extensively since
(a) **1960's** (b) 1970's
(c) 1980's (d) 1990's.

53. The arrangement of catalogue entries in a logical and systematic order to fall into a helpful sequence for strong and retrieval is referred to as
(a) Card form (b) Alphabetical form
(c) **Classified form** (d) Inner form.

54. Which catalogue is a variation and extension of an author catalogue?
(a) Classified catalogue (b) **Name catalogue**
(c) Alphabetical catalogue (d) Author catalogue.

55. The British Museum Cataloguing Rules is also known as
(a) Baber's Rules (b) **Panizzi's Rules**
(c) Vatican Rules (d) Jewett's Rules.

56. AACRII was published in
(a) 1967 (b) 1974
(c) **1978** (d) 1988.

57. To direct the user of a catalogue from a form of the name of a person or a corporate body or the title of a work that might reasonably be sought to the form that has been chosen as a name heading or a uniform title is the function of a
(a) **See reference** (b) See also reference
(c) Cross reference (d) Direct reference.

58. The system in which the main entry and added entries carry the same information about the document is known as
(a) MARC Card System (b) **Unit Card System**
(c) Single Card System (d) Integrated Card System.

59. Which section in the CCC is that section which records authorship or its substitute element?
(a) **Heading section** (b) Leading section
(c) Title section (d) Author section.

60. A record of all additional entries is known as
(a) Unit Card (b) Book Index Entry
(c) Tracing (d) **Added Entry**.

61. In CCC, Class Index Entry consists of successively the following sections a) heading section b) second section, and c)
(a) call number (b) **index number**
(c) class number (d) book number.

62. ALA filing Rules was first published in

(a) 1968 (b) **1942**
(c) 1961 (d) 1956.

63. Which Filing Rules has their origins in the report of a Working Party on Computer Filing set up by the Library Association Cataloguing and Indexing Group?
(a) **BLAISE** (b) LC
(c) ALA (d) Berghoeffer.

64. The structure of the main entry according to AACR-2R consists of
(a) four parts (b) five parts
(c) six parts (d) **eight parts**.

65. According to the needs of a document and needs of a particular Library, AACR, prescribed
(a) one level of description
(b) two levels of description
(c) **three levels of description**
(d) four levels of description.

66. In Bibliographic data formats, codes used to identify different data elements in the record viz., author, title, scale of map, starting dates of journals etc. is known as
(a) Record label (b) Directory
(c) Data fields (d) **Content designator**.

67. CCF stands for
(a) Current Classification Format
(b) Current Communication Format
(c) **Common Communication Format**
(d) Common Classification Format.

68. Each CCF record begins with a fixed length label of
(a) 4 characters (b) 20 characters
(c) **24 characters** (d) 16 characters.

69. GMD in AACR-2R stands for
(a) General Material Description
(b) **General Material Designation**
(c) Geographical Material Description
(d) General Monographic Designation.

70. The internationally agreed upon number given to a book is known as
    (a) ISSN (b) ISBD
    (c) **ISBN** (d) ISCN.
71. Cutter Number or Cutter Mark is used for
    (a) Call number (b) **Book number**
    (c) Class number (d) Collection number.
72. In AACR-2R, the courts are entered under their
    (a) **Jurisdiction**
    (b) Name directly
    (c) Name of the Chief Justice
    (d) Name of the government.
73. In CCC, Conferences and Congresses are entered under the
    (a) name of the sponsor
    (b) name of the place where it is held
    (c) **name by which they are known**
    (d) under the country name.
74. In AACR-2R the anonymous works of personal authors are to be entered under
    (a) **Title** (b) Editor
    (c) Subject (d) Collaborator.
75. Which lists within its frame all bibliographic elements, which are required to describe and identify all types of materials, which are likely to appear in library collection?
    (a) MARC lists (b) CCF lists
    (c) UNIMARC lists (d) **ISBD (G) lists**.
76. According to AACR-2R, chief source of information for microforms is
    (a) title page (b) container box
    (c) **title frame** (d) container and label.
77. Three types of analytical entries in CCC are author analytical, title analytical and
    (a) series analytical (b) **subject analytical**
    (c) name analytical (d) edition analytical.

78. According to AACR-2R, collections of treaties between two parties are to be entered under
(a) Title **(b) Uniform title**
(c) country name (d) Signing parties.

79. Containing more than one unit concept in them and a number of terms may be used to fully describe these concepts is called as
(a) **Multi work concept** (b) Complex subject
(c) compound subject (d) Meta subject.

80. How many rules for treatment of pseudonyms in CCC?
(a) **5** (b) 10
(c) 15 (d) 20.

81. Subject headings lists and thesauri are two types of
(a) natural indexing language
(b) free indexing language
(c) **controlled indexing language**
(d) uncontrolled indexing language.

82. Which system contain tools which will automatically create classified listing of the resource and a search mechanism for Internet resources?
(a) Prompt cat (b) First Search
(c) **ROADS** (d) World Cat.

83. Computer Aided Subject System (COMPASS) was introduced in 1991 for
(a) INB (b) ABPR
(c) Books in Print (d) **BNB**.

CLASSIFICATION THEORY

1. Colon Classification (Ed.7) is
(a) an enumerative scheme
(b) an almost faceted scheme
(c) a rigidly faceted scheme
(d) **a freely faceted scheme**.

2. Table 3 in DDC I9th ed. stands for
(a) standard subdivision (b) language divisions
(c) group of persons (d) **literature subdivision**.

3. The concept of 'Emptying Digit' facilitates
   (a) hospitality in chain (b) **interpolation in array**
   (c) extrapolation in array (d) interpolation in chain.
4. In the class no.22;46:51.44 the digits 46 represent
   (a) personality (b) energy
   (c) **matter** (d) space.
5. The Index given in the DDC is called
   (a) an analytical index (b) **relative index**
   (c) subject index (d) co-ordinate index.
6. Complex subjects are formed by
   (a) Fission (b) Lamination
   (c) **Loose Assemblage** (d) Distillation.
7. 20th edition of DDC is in
   (a) 1 volume (b) 2 volumes
   (c) 3 volumes (d) **4 volumes**.
8. Melvil Dewey was the propounder of
   (a) dichotomy (b) **decachotomy**
   (c) polychotomy (d) none of these.
9. Library of Congress Classification was devised by
   (a) S. R. Ranganathan (b) C. A. Cutter
   (c) H. E. Bliss (d) **a corporate body**.
10. DDC is a
    (a) freely faceted schedule
    (b) almost faceted schedule
    (c) rigidly faceted schedule
    (d) **phoenix schedule**.
11. Bibliographic classification scheme was devised by
    (a) W.C. B. Sayers (b) E. C. Richardson
    (c) F. W. Lancaster (d) **H. E. Bliss**.
12. In UDC, to combine the facets, the facet indicators used are
    (a) colon
    (b) double colon
    (c) square bracket
    (d) **colon, double colon, square bracket**.

13. 20th edition of DDC is in
    (a) 1 volume (b) 2 volumes
    (c) 3 volumes (d) **4 volumes**.
14. Library of Congress Classification was devised by
    (a) S. R. Ranganathan (b) C. A. Cutter
    (c) H. E. Bliss (d) **a corporate body**.
15. DDC is a
    (a) freely faceted schedule
    (b) almost faceted schedule
    (c) rigidly faceted schedule
    (d) **phoenix schedule**.
16. Bibliographic classification scheme was devised by
    (a) W.C. B. Sayers (b) E. C. Richardson
    (c) F. W. Lancaster (d) **H. E. Bliss**.
17. Broad System of Ordering is a
    (a) cataloguing system (b) indexing system
    (c) abstracting system (d) **classification system**.
18. 'Statistical method' is formed with
    (a) loose assemblage mode
    (b) cluster mode
    (c) **distillation mode**
    (d) fission mode.
19. 'Tree of Porphyry' is a schematic representation of
    (a) decachotomy (b) **dichotomy**
    (c) polychotomy (d) anatomy.
20. The theory of 'Literary Warrant' was enunciated by
    (a) B. C. Vickery (b) M. A. Gopinath
    (c) S. Seetharama (d) **E. W. Hulme**.
21. Mnemonics means
    (a) division (b) subdivision
    (c) standard subdivision (d) **aid to memory**.
22. Enumerative classification means
    (a) classification scheme providing class number of necessary facets
    (b) classification scheme providing class number of broad subjects

(c) classification scheme providing class number of complex subjects
(d) **classification scheme providing readymade class numbers for all subjects of past, present and anticipatable future.**

23. Mode of formation of subject 'oceanography' is
(a) fission (b) fusion
(c) lamination (d) **cluster.**

24. P-notes are used for revision of
(a) DDC (b) **UDC**
(c) CC (d) BC.

25. Notation as 'a shorthand sign' was defined by
(a) S. R. Ranganathan (b) W. C. B. Sayers
(c) **E. C. Richardson** (d) M. Bates.

26. DDC 19th edition is an
(a) freely faceted scheme
(b) rigidly faceted scheme
(c) fully enumerated scheme
(d) **almost enumerative scheme.**

27. The Classification Research Group has its headquarters at
(a) India (b) New York
(c) Netherlands (d) **London.**

28. Principle of Osmosis is concerned with
(a) cataloguing (b) classification
(c) **re-classification** (d) re-cataloguing.

29. Colon Classification provides schedule for
(a) ACI (b) **PCI**
(c) NCI (d) FCI.

30. Colon Classification was first published in
(a) 1932 (b) **1933**
(c) 1934 (d) 1935.

31. In Colon Classification the class number for a system is devised by
(a) input devices (b) output devices
(c) technical devices (d) **chronological devices.**

32. The common isolates in UDC are called
    (a) main tables (b) sub tables
    (c) standard tables (d) **auxiliary tables**.
33. In the notational system of a classification scheme an 'empty digit' denotes that has
    (a) no real value (b) **no semantic value**
    (c) no syntactical value (d) none of these.
34. The modes of formation of the subject 'Research Methodology' is
    (a) loose assemblage (b) lamination
    (c) fission (d) **distillation**.
35. In classification, the sequence of two isolate ideas in an array is determined by the
    (a) principle of filiatory sequence
    (b) principle of array
    (c) principle of chain
    (d) **principle of facet sequence**.
36. Universal Decimal Classification system was tested in the
    (a) Hawthorn experiment
    (b) IFLA experiment
    (c) IASLIC experiment
    (d) **ASLIB-Cranfield experiment**.
37. The fundamental category 'time' is considered as
    (a) most concrete element (b) **least concrete element**
    (c) most abstract element (d) least abstract element.
38. Wall – picture principle helps in deciding
    (a) isolate sequence
    (b) complex subject sequence
    (c) compound subject sequence
    (d) **facet sequence**.
39. The DDC was first published in
    (a) 1877 (b) 1878
    (c) **1876** (d) 1879.
40. The author of 'Prolegomena of Library Classification' is

(a) W. C. B. Sayers (b) E. C. Richardson
(c) H. E. Bliss (d) **S. R. Ranganathan**.

41. In chain procedure Class Index Entry is derived from
(a) book number (b) call number
(c) **class number** (d) index number.

42. According to S. R. Ranganathan's principles and postulates, the sequence of component ideas in the subject 'the effects of radiation treatment of lung cancer' is
(a) lung, cancer, treatment, medicine, radiation, effects
(b) **medicine, lung, cancer, treatment, radiation, effects**
(c) lung, cancer, medicine, treatment, radiation, effects
(d) medicine, treatment, lung, cancer, radiation, effects.

43. The process by which a library can identify 'active' collection for reprocessing is
(a) principle of later in evolution
(b) principle of earlier in evolution
(c) **principle of osmosis**
(d) principle of oasis.

44. Not a principle of facet sequence is
(a) **principle of later in evolution**
(b) whole organ principle
(c) cow-calf principle
(d) Act and- Action-Actor-Tool principle

45. Intra facet phase relation is used for representing relationship between
(a) **two isolates belonging to the same facet**
(b) two isolates belonging to the different facets
(c) three isolates belonging to the same facets
(d) three isolates belonging to the different facets.

46. The mode of formation involved in the subject 'Indology' is

(a) fission (b) fusion
(c) distillation (d) **cluster**.

47. CC6 is a
(a) rigidly faceted classification scheme
(b) almost faceted classification scheme
(c) enumerative classification scheme
(d) **freely faceted classification scheme**.

48. According to CC the title 'Psychology for Doctors' is an example of
(a) intra array phase relation
(b) intra facet phase relation
(c) **inter subject phase relation**
(d) intra subject phase relation.

49. Subject formed with a basic subject and one or more isolate idea defined as
(a) basic subject (b) complex subject
(c) **compound subject** (d) none of these.

50. Hospitality in chain can be secured by
(a) mnemonic devices
(b) gap devices
(c) **gap and fractional devices**
(d) input devices.

51. The sign used to indicate all types of phase and facet relation in UDC is
(a) double colon (b) **colon**
(c) square bracket (d) double inverted comma.

52. The concept of common isolates was formulated by
(a) W. C. B. Sayers (b) C. A. Cutter
(c) **S. R. Ranganathan** (d) H. E. Bliss.

53. The subject 'Biochemistry' is the result of
(a) loose assemblage mode of formation
(b) lamination mode of formation
(c) fission mode of formation
(d) **fusion mode of formation**.

54. 'Biotechnology' is an example of how knowledge grows by

(a) **Fusion** (b) Lamination
(c) Fission (d) Loose Assemblage.

55. In a classification scheme the groups Special Libraries, Medical Libraries, Hospital Libraries represent
(a) A Facet (b) An Array
(c) **A Chain** (d) A Characteristics.

56. Emptying digit device is used in CC to provide for
(a) **Hospitality in Array**
(b) Hospitality in Chain
(c) Alternative Arrangement
(d) Flexibility.

57. What is the edition of CC in which the fundamental categories were introduced for the first time?
(a) 2nd (b) **3rd**
(c) 5th (d) 6th.

58. In a classification scheme for persons, the following groups are created on the basis of age: Infants, Children, Adolescents & Adults. Age represents
(a) **an array** (b) a facet
(c) a chain (d) none of these.

59. Statement 'A': All faceted scheme of classification need not be analytico synthetic. Statement B: All analytico-synthetic schemes are facet.
(a) **both statements are correct**
(b) only statement A is correct
(c) only statement B is correct
(d) both statements are incorrect.

60. Phase relation may have to be shown at the
(a) subject level (b) facet level
(c) array level (d) **all of the above**.

61. The topic "statistical methods for the social sciences" is an example of
(a) lamination (b) **loose assemblage**
(c) fission (d) fusion.

62. A system of terms used to denote the classes or ranked isolates in a scheme for classification is called as
(a) Thesaurus (b) **terminology**
(c) concepts (d) vocabulary.

63. The terminology of library classification is a/an
(a) **interactive terminology**
(b) ordinary terminology
(c) intrinsic terminology
(d) basic terminology.

64. Which terms define the basic concepts germane to the very nature of classification process?
(a) Normative terms (b) **Fundamental terms**
(c) Associative terms (d) Assumed terms.

65. Classification in Sense 2 is
(a) Division (b) **Assortment**
(c) Entity (d) Universe.

66. Any property or quantitative measure or quality possessed by or inherent in an entity is defined as
(a) **Attribute** (b) Characteristic
(c) Universe (d) Class.

67. Detailed Classification required for Micro documents is known as
(a) library classification (b) book classification
(c) broad classification (d) **depth classification**.

68. The subject of the document whose extension and intension are equal to the thought content of the document is defined as
(a) **specific subject** (b) basic subject
(c) broad subject (d) depth subject.

69. A traditional subdivision of an old main class is known as a
(a) traditional class (b) **canonical class**
(c) system main class (d) special main class.

70. The process of analysing a complex subject into its constituent phases is known as a
(a) Facet Analysis (b) Array Analysis

(c) **Phase Analysis** (d) Isolate Analysis.

71. On the basis of common characteristics isolates are grouped in
    (a) sequence (b) array
    (c) category (d) **facet**.

72. Broader groups in an array are arranged in
    (a) evolutionary sequence
    (b) parallel sequence
    (c) **filiatory sequence**
    (d) helpful sequence.

73. The Classification in which all classes and their corresponding symbols are listed is defined as
    (a) **Enumerative Classification**
    (b) Faceted Classification
    (c) Freely Faceted Classification
    (d) Rigidly Faceted Classification.

74. The total number of species of digits used in the notational system of CC is
    (a) **six** (b) ten
    (c) three (d) fourteen.

75. In CC (7th edn.) the digits asterisk, plus, double inverted comma and backward arrow have
    (a) positive value (b) **anteriorising value**
    (c) posteriorising value (d) negative value.

76. Any number in a notational system is denoted as
    (a) symbol (b) **notation**
    (c) digit (d) array.

77. Placing closely related subjects in close proximity in a scheme of classification is called
    (a) **filiatory sequence** (b) parallel sequence
    (c) collocation (d) helpful sequence.

78. How many stages are in the development of the general theory of library classification?
    (a) **two** (b) three
    (c) four (d) seven.

79. Who evolved a Dynamic Theory of Classification?

(a) Hulme and his associates
(b) Richardson and his associates
(c) Brown and his associates
(d) **Ranganathan and his associates.**

80. Which Classification Scheme spring from some definite source?
(a) **Subject Classification**
(b) International Classification
(c) Decimal Classification
(d) Bibliographic Classification.

81. Who is regarded as the first classificationists to have made a systematicattempt to set down a theory of library classification?
(a) Hulme (b) Brown
(c) **Richardson** (d) Sayers.

82. Who said that all classifications could be arranged into two groups, i.e., Mechanical and Physical?
(a) Sayers (b) **Hulme**
(c) Ranganathan (d) Brown.

83. Which means a subject in a classification scheme is given two alternative places?
(a) **Alternative Location** (b) Parallel Location
(c) Collocation (d) Literary Warrant.

84. Arranging subjects in the order of decreasing extension in a scheme of classification is called
(a) **subordination** (b) co-extensiveness
(c) coordinate classes (d) division.

85. Ranganathan's Colon Classification is an excellent example of
(a) Enumerative Classification
(b) Facet Classification
(c) Fully Faceted Classification
(d) **Freely Faceted Analytico Synthetic Classification.**

86. Rider's International Classification is
(a) Faceted Classification

(b) Freely Faceted Classification
(c) **Enumerative Classification**
(d) Almost Enumerative Classification.

87. In 1978 FID was published Third Edition of
(a) BC (b) **BSO**
(c) LC (d) UDC.

88. Which classification systems are detailed classification meant to classify micro literature?
(a) **Special Classification**
(b) Broad Classification
(c) Book Classification
(d) Bibliographic Classification.

89. In India the Special Schedules for classification have been designed by
(a) DESIDOC (b) INSDOC
(c) **DRTC** (d) NASSDOC.

90. Universe of Subjects is ever growing and, therefore,
(a) translation is ever growing
(b) documentation is ever growing
(c) library science is ever growing
(d) **library service s ever growing**.

91. Which mode is assembling together of two or more of a) subjects b) isolate ideas?
(a) Lamination (b) **Loose Assemblage**
(c) Fission (d) Fusion.

92. Area Study, Generalia Person Study and Study of Entity or Phenomena are some of the examples of
(a) Lamination (b) Fusion
(c) Fission (d) **Clustering**.

93. Ranganathan's approach to the structuring of subjects is based on
(a) **postulational approach**
(b) mnemonic approach
(c) theoretical approach
(d) practical approach.

94. Expressive title which is also called

(a) Raw title (b) **Full title**
(c) Kernel title (d) Analysed title.

95. Isolates such as variance, intensity, wave length, height, weight, volume, etc. are regarded as manifestation of
(a) Personality (b) **Matter**
(c) Energy (d) Time and Space.

96. Which is the central part of the whole subject, encompassing a range of related ideas?
(a) Space (b) Time
(c) Energy (d) **Personality**.

97. Which is an aspect of a subject?
(a) **Facet** (b) Isolate
(c) Category (d) Postulate.

98. Different levels of the same fundamental category within a round of facets in a compound subject should be kept together comes under the Postulate of
(a) level (b) **level cluster**
(c) concreteness (d) first facet.

99. Subject is formed by a combination of two or more subjects called as
(a) Basic subject (b) Compound subject
(c) **Complex subject** (d) Specific subject.

100. In the influence phase relation the subject that is influenced is the
(a) **first phase by the subject that influences**
(b) second phase by the subject that influences
(c) primary phase by the subject that influences
(d) secondary phase by the subject that influences.

101. Statistics for Engineers, and Mathematics for Economics are the examples of
(a) general phase relation
(b) influence phase relation
(c) **bias phase relation**
(d) comparison phase relation.

102. In UDC, Common Isolates are called
   (a) **auxiliary subdivisions**
   (b) common subdivisions
   (c) special subdivisions
   (d) form subdivisions.
103. In CC, Bibliography, Concordance, Tale, Atlas are some of the ACI which are applicable before
   (a) time facet in the class number
   (b) **space facet in the class number**
   (c) energy facet in the class number
   (d) personality facet in the class number.
104. In DDC 19th edition a complete list of Standard Subdivisions appear in volume1 as Table
   (a) **1** (b) 2
   (c) 3 (d) 3A.
105. In UDC the common auxiliaries of form are put in parentheses with a connecting symbol
   (a) **double inverted comma**
   (b) ampersand
   (c) nought
   (d) comma.
106. The electronic version of DDC 21 (1996), named
   (a) Computerised Dewey (b) Electronic Dewey
   (c) Dewey on CD (d) **Dewey for Windows**.
107. The responsibility for the maintenance and updating of UDC lies with
   (a) ALA (b) LA
   (c) IFLA (d) **FID**.
108. In 1951, S. R. Ranganathan was founded
   (a) CRG (b) **LRC**
   (c) FID/CA (d) ISKO.
109. Add to device is one of the synthetic devices in
   (a) CC (b) LC
   (c) BC (d) **DDC**.
110. A mark borne by a book that denotes its exact or fixed position on a shelf is called

(a) Interfile (b) Shelf mark
(c) **Book mark** (d) Class mark.

111. Who defined 'Notation as a shorthand sign'?
(a) **E.C.Richardson** (b) S.R.Ranganathan
(c) W.C.B.Sayers (d) C.A.Cutter.

112. Geopolitics formed by the mode of
(a) fission (b) **fusion**
(c) cluster (d) loose assemblage.

113. Who was the first grammarian of library classification?
(a) E.C.Richardson (b) **W.C.B.Sayers**
(c) S.R.Ranganathan (d) C.A.Cutter.

114. Who adopted the 'One Place' theory?
(a) **James Duff Brown** (b) S.R.Ranganathan
(c) E.W.Hulme (d) F.W.Lancaster.

115. Who wrote 'Principles of Book Classification'?
(a) **E.W.Hulme** (b) W.C.B.Sayers
(c) S.R.Ranganathan (d) Thomas Childers.

116. Who used first the word 'canon'?
(a) **W.C.B.Sayers** (b) James Duff Brown
(c) E.W.Hulme (d) C.A.Cutter.

117. Sayer's canon of classification appeared in which year?
(a) 1910 (b) **1915**
(c) 1916 (d) 1918.

118. In which year Sayer's 'Introduction to library classification' was published?
(a) 1908 (b) 1911
(c) 1917 (d) **1918**.

119. In which year Sayer's 'Manual of Classification' was published?
(a) 1916 (b) 1918
(c) 1925 (d) **1926**.

120. Who defined 'A notation is a symbol of marks...things'?
(a) **H.E.Bliss** (b) S.R.Ranganathan
(c) W.C.B.Sayers (d) C.A.Cutter.

121. Who defined 'A number forming a member of notational system'?

(a) **S.R.Ranganathan** (b) H.E.Bliss
(c) E.W.Hulme (d) C.A.Cutter.

122. In which year 'Prolegomena to library classification' was published?
(a) **1949** (b) 1948
(c) 1947 (d) 1946.

123. Who wrote the book 'Classification, theoretical and practical'?
(a) **E.C.Richardson** (b) E.W.Hulme
(c) S.R.Ranganathan (d) W.C.B.Sayers.

124. In which year the book 'Classification, theoretical and practical' was published?
(a) **1901** (b) 1902
(c) 1903 (d) 1904.

125. In which year UDC abridged edition was published?
(a) 1962 (b) 1963
(c) **1961** (d) 1964.

126. In which year UDC International Medium edition (BS1000M) was published?
(a) **1985** (b) 1986
(c) 1987 (d) 1988.

127. Who wrote the book 'Organization of knowledge in library science and the subject approach to books'?
(a) D.J.Fosket (b) E.W.Hulme
(c) **H.E.Bliss** (d) E.C.Richardson.

128. Who wrote 'Nayakosa'?
(a) A.C.Foskett (b) H.E.Bliss
(c) D.J.Foskett (d) **S.R.Ranganathan**.

129. Who wrote the book 'Manual of library classification and self arrangement'?
(a) **J.D.Brown** (b) E.C.Richardson
(c) E.W.Hulme (d) S.R.Ranganathan.

130. What are the two parts of UDC abridged edition?
(a) main tables and index
(b) main tables and relative index
(c) syntagmatic tables and relative index

(d) **syntagmatic tables and index**.

131. Who wrote the book 'Essentials of library classification'?
(a) **S.R.Ranganathan** (b) E.W.Hulme
(c) C.A.Cutter (d) A.C.Foskett.

132. In which place and year 1st International study Conference on Classificatiion Research held?
(a) **Dorking (1957)** (b) Elsinore (1964)
(c) Mumbai (1975) (d) Augsberg (1982).

133. How many entries belong to DDC18?
(a) **26141** (b) 26142
(c) 26143 (d) 26144.

134. Who wrote the book 'Manual of Classification for librarians and bibliographers'?
(a) **W.C.B.Sayers** (b) E.C. Richardson
(c) E.W.Hulme (d) S.R.Ranganathan.

135. Who wrote 'Introduction to cataloguing and classification of books'?
(a) **Margaret Mann** (b) C.A.Cutter
(c) A.C.Foskett (d) D.J.Foskett.

136. In which year BSO concept took place?
(a) 1969 (b) 1970
(c) **1971** (d) 1972

137. Who is/are the inventor(s) of BSO concept?
(a) **UNESCO/ICSU** (b) IFLA
(c) ALA (d) LA.

138. In which year BSO 1st edition published by whom?
(a) **1978** (b) 1979
(c) 1980 (d) 1981.

139. In which year BSO manual published?
(a) 1978 (b) **1979**
(c) 1980 (d) 1981.

140. Who was the propounder of 'Dichotomy'?
(a) Melvil Dewey (b) **Immanuel Kant**
(c) A.C.Foskett (d) C.A.Cutter.

141. Who was the propounder of 'Polychotomy'?

(a) **C.A.Cutter** (b) D.J.Foskett
(c) Tom Childers (d) Derek Austin.

DOCUMENTATION THEORY

1. Full form of SENDOC is
   (a) Seminar on National Documentation
   (b) Small Entrepreneurs Documentation Centre
   (c) Small Enterprises Documentation
   (d) **Small Enterprises National Documentation Centre**.
2. Biological Abstracts have five indexes viz. Generic, Basic, Cross, Bio-systematic and
   (a) Editor (b) Compiler
   (c) Series Editor (d) **Author**.
3. The method of deriving class index entries through chain procedure was devised by
   (a) Ganesh Bhattacharyya
   (b) **S. R. Ranganathan**
   (c) M. A. Gopinath
   (d) P. N. Kaula.
4. 'Current Contents' is brought out by
   (a) ILA
   (b) IASLIC
   (c) LA
   (d) **Institute for Scientific Information, Philadelphia**.
5. BNB is at present deriving subject index entries according to
   (a) POPSI (b) KWIC
   (c) KWOC (d) **PRECIS**.
6. Headquarters of FID is located at
   (a) India (b) Denmark
   (c) Sweden (d) **The Hague**.
7. FID now stands for
   (a) International Federation for Documentation

(b) International Federation for Database
(c) International Federation for Development
(d) **International Federation for Information and Documentation.**

8. NASSDOC is an organ of
(a) INSDOC (b) SENDOC
(c) DRTC (d) **ICSSR.**

9. POPSI was conceived by
(a) Ganesh Bhattacharyya
(b) **S. R. Ranganathan**
(c) M. A. Gopinath
(d) S. Seetharama.

10. Indian Science Abstracts is being published by
(a) DRTC (b) ICSSR
(c) INFLIBNET (d) **INSDOC.**

11. SDI is associated with the name of
(a) S. R. Ranganathan (b) H. E. Bliss
(c) C. A. Cutter (d) **H. P. Luhn.**

12. The concept of co-ordinate indexing was developed by
(a) Ganesh Bhattacharyya (b) Martia Bates
(c) Blaise Cronin (d) **Mortimer Taube.**

13. In 'SDI' document characteristics are matched with
(a) information needs profiles
(b) information seeking behaviour profiles
(c) information services profiles
(d) **user profiles.**

14. The practice of consulting the colleagues and seeking information at the needed hour is known as
(a) invisible information (b) invisible sights
(c) invisible users (d) **invisible colleagues.**

15. Chemical Abstracts is published by
(a) American Biological Society
(b) American Sociological Society
(c) American Anthropological Society
(d) **American Chemical Society.**

16. The basic difference between SDI and other modes of current awareness is that SDI is
    (a) directed towards the needs of a group of users
    (b) directed towards the needs of all users
    (c) **directed towards the needs of an individual user/project**
    (d) none of these.
17. Routing of journals (Content by Journals) is related to
    (a) **Current Awareness Service**
    (b) Selective Dissemination of Service
    (c) Abstracting
    (d) Indexing.
18. In computer based system, commonly used indexing language is
    (a) co-ordinate indexing language
    (b) keyword indexing language
    (c) **free indexing language**
    (d) none of these.
19. The union catalogue of Social Science Serials in India brought out by
    (a) INSDOC (b) **NASSDOC**
    (c) SENDOC (d) DRTC.
20. Non- conventional approach of subject indexing is
    (a) pre-coordinate indexing
    (b) post-coordinate indexing
    (c) chain indexing
    (d) **citation indexing**.
21. DRTC is located in
    (a) Delhi (b) Mumbai
    (c) Kolkata (d) **Bangalore**.
22. Science Citation Index is a publication of
    (a) ALA
    (b) American Chemical Society
    (c) American Biological Society
    (d) **Institute for Scientific Information, Philadelphia (1964, 5 vols.)**.

23. 'Library Literature' is a
(a) abstracting periodical (b) **indexing periodical**
(c) serials (d) encyclopedia.

24. Paul Otlet and Henry La Fontain were instrumental for establishment of
(a) IFLA (b) **FID**
(c) ASLIB (d) ALA.

25. SENDOC aims at catering information needs of
(a) large scale industries (b) a community
(c) scholars (d) **small scale industries**.

26. The premier institution for prescribing standards in India is
(a) ISI (b) ANSI
(c) SSI (d) **BIS**.

27. Providing latest information to research scholars/ scientists and others on their research work is through
(a) SDI (b) **CAS**
(c) indexing (d) abstracting.

28. National Science Library of India is located at
(a) ISI, Kolkata (b) IIT, Kharagpur
(c) INSDOC (d) **IIS, Bangalore**.

29. National Index of Translations is published by
(a) NASSDOC (b) DRTC
(c) **INSDOC** (d) ILA.

30. POPSI is an
(a) indexing system of author entries
(b) indexing system of title entries
(c) indexing system of editor entries
(d) **indexing system of subject entries**.

31. Periodicity of Chemical Abstract is
(a) fortnightly (b) monthly
(c) quarterly (d) **weekly**.

32. Secondary sources are created to facilitate access to information contents of
(a) secondary sources
(b) **primary sources**

(c) tertiary sources
(d) primary and secondary sources.

33. Periodical articles are
(a) secondary sources (b) tertiary sources
(c) **primary sources** (d) none of these.

34. National Translation Services in India is located at
(a) NISSAT (b) **INSDOC**
(c) DESIDOC (d) NASSDOC.

35. The originator of 'Science Citation Index' is
(a) **Eugene Garfield** (b) Farradane
(c) H. P. Luhn (d) W. C. B. Sayers.

36. In which of the following types of Indexes are access points not derived automatically
(a) KWIC (b) Citation Indexing
(c) KWOC (d) **POPSI**.

37. KWIC indexing technique is based on
(a) **Titles** (b) Citations
(c) Abstracts (d) Full Text.

38. MESH is an example of
(a) classification scheme (b) **thesaurus**
(c) abstracting journal (d) classaurus.

39. A 'slanted abstract' is
(a) a critical evaluation of an article
(b) **one that is written for a specific group of users**
(c) an abstract of a biased article
(d) none of these.

40. Post co-ordinate indexes overcomes difficulties created by
(a) **fixed citation order** (b) synonymous terms
(c) time taken (d) inconsistencies.

41. Among the following which is a NISSAT sectoral centre?
(a) National Chemical Laboratory
(b) National Information Centre
(c) **Central Drug Research Institute**

(d) Ahmedabad Textile Industries Research Association.

42. SENDOC is a documentation centre on

(a) steel enterprise (b) **small scale industries**

(c) stock exchange (d) sugar industries.

43. "Half life" of information implies

(a) **information is useful only half the time** (b) an information ages, it is used less

(c) the life of information is reduced

(d) dead information is not used.

44. "Grey literature" means

(a) documents which are bound in grey cloth

(b) literature which contains classified information

(c) **literature which is semi-published**

(d) literature which is to be published in future.

45. Which of the following cannot be considered as a primary source of information?

(a) an article describing original research

(b) **a text book**

(c) a patent

(d) a thesis.

46. Conference proceedings are considered as

(a) conventional documents

(b) **primary documents**

(c) secondary documents

(d) tertiary documents.

47. Who divides documents into three types such as primary, secondary and tertiary?

(a) **Grogan** (b) J. S. Mills

(c) J. H. Shera (d) P. V. Young.

48. What type of information was provided by pamphlets?

(a) Obsolete (b) **Current**

(c) Traditional (d) Conventional.

49. ISI has been renamed as

(a) NBT (b) **BIS**

(c) ILA (d) ISO.

50. Which documents provide information on the processes and materials involved in the manufacture of a product?
    (a) **Patents** (b) Standards
    (c) Specifications (d) Trade Literature.
51. Institutional and human resources are known as
    (a) biographical sources of information
    (b) government sources of information
    (c) documentary sources of information
    (d) **non-documentary sources of information.**
52. What is the central character in Drury's principle of book selection?
    (a) staff (b) **reader**
    (c) library collection (d) building.
53. A critical evaluation of book is made through
    (a) **book review** (b) library review
    (c) newspaper (d) review digest.
54. A limited set of terms that must be used to index documents in a particular system refers to
    (a) Indexing (b) Indexing System
    (c) **Vocabulary Control** (d) Subject Heading.
55. The concept of 'Thesauro Facet' has been developed by
    (a) Derek Austin (b) Ganesh Bhattacharya
    (c) Ranganathan (d) **Jean Atchison**.
56. The indexing system in which coordination of terms in the index descriptions are decided before any particular request is made, is known as
    (a) co-ordinate indexing system
    (b) post-coordinate indexing system
    (c) descriptive indexing system
    (d) **pre-coordinate indexing system**.
57. POPSI is an example of
    (a) post-coordinate indexing model
    (b) **pre-coordinate indexing model**
    (c) natural indexing model
    (d) free indexing model.

58. The synonymous relationship between the terms is known as
    (a) hierarchical relationship
    (b) genus-species relationship
    (c) associate relationship
    (d) **equivalent relationship**.
59. KWAC stands for
    (a) Keyword Associate Context
    (b) **Keyword And Context**
    (c) Keyword Abbreviated Context
    (d) Keyword And Context.
60. The type of user's approach in which a user may want to look all the information that have been published on a given topic is known as
    (a) **Everyday Approach** (b) Current Approach
    (c) Exhaustive Approach (d) Catching up Approach.
61. Which approach is essential to every active professional to keep abreast of the latest developments in his field and also to every researcher to avoid duplication of research effort?
    (a) Everyday approach (b) Exhaustive approach
    (c) **Current approach** (d) Catching up approach.
62. Which is essentially distinguishes between information source and resource?
    (a) **The idea of organization for reuse**
    (b) The idea of use of raw material
    (c) The idea of procuring the raw material
    (d) The idea of dissemination of information.
63. The information services to the users can be grouped under
    (a) **two categories** (b) three categories
    (c) four categories (d) five categories.
64. When the reference personnel do the search on behalf of the user, it is known as
    (a) direct search (b) **delegated search**
    (c) self search (d) user search.

65. SDI stands for
(a) Selective Documentation of Information
(b) Subject Dissemination
(c) Specific Document of Information
(d) **Selective Dissemination of Information**.

66. SDI service is one form of
(a) **current awareness service**
(b) reference service
(c) literature search service
(d) referral service.

67. Which services do not aid the user to keep abreast of developments in any specific subject field, but enable him to find solution to a particular problem?
(a) Current awareness services
(b) Retrospective search services
(c) **SDI services**
(d) Anticipatory search services.

68. IACs stands for
(a) Indian Abstracting Centres
(b) Information Addition Centres
(c) **Information Analysis Centres**
(d) Indian Analysis Centres.

69. Cambridge Crystallographic Data Centre is an example of
(a) Documentation centre
(b) Referral centre
(c) Reference centre
(d) **Data analysis centre**.

70. Selection, evaluation, validation, standardization, summarisation, and synthesis of information are the processes for
(a) abstracting (b) indexing
(c) literature search (d) **information analysis**.

71. Indian Institute of Science is located at
(a) New Delhi (b) Mumbai
(c) Kolkata (d) **Bangalore**.

72. The indexing and abstracting publication belong to the
    (a) primary publication group
    (b) **secondary publication group**
    (c) tertiary publication group
    (d) reference publication group.
73. The National Translation Centre (USA)brings out
    (a) World Transindex
    (b) Translations Register-Index
    (c) **Index Translationum**
    (d) National Translation Index.
74. Document Delivery Service is sometimes referred to as
    (a) SDI service (b) Abstracting service
    (c) **Back-up service** (d) Literature search service.
75. Right Pages and Science Direct is a type of
    (a) abstracting service
    (b) altering service
    (c) **document delivery service**
    (d) publication service.
76. Newspaper clipping service is a type of
    (a) **anticipatory information service**
    (b) responsive information service
    (c) on demand reference
    (d) retrospective information service.
77. Which files comprise of a complete documentation of information available in journals, reports, conference papers and similar publications in the subject areas of projects?
    (a) Project specification (b) Project execution
    (c) **Project information** (d) Government project.

INFORMATION SOURCES & SERVICES

1. DELNET is a
   (a) **wide area network** (b) local area network
   (c) national network (d) regional network.
2. British Library Automated Information Services (BLAISE) is useful in the field of
   (a) Biochemistry (b) **Biomedicine**
   (c) Biophysics (d) Biology.
3. NICNET is a project sponsored by
   (a) **Government of India** (b) UGC
   (c) INFLIBNET (d) NISSAT.
4. AGRIS is mainly sponsored by
   (a) ICAR (b) IFLA
   (c) **UNISIST & FAO** (d) UNESCO.
5. INFLIBNET stands for
   (a) Informing Library Network
   (b) Information and Librarians Network
   (c) **Information and Library Network**
   (d) Indian National Frontier Library Network.
6. The library network mainly for university libraries in India is known as
   (a) CALIBNET (b) MALIBNET
   (c) **INFLIBNET** (d) DELNET.
7. National Information Centre on Chemistry and Chemical Technology (NICCHEM) is located at
   (a) **Pune** (b) Lucknow
   (c) Hyderabad (d) Bangalore.
8. NICDAP stands for
   (a) National Information Centre for Data Access Programmeming
   (b) National Information Centre for Document Access Programmeming
   (c) National Information Centre for Development and Programmeming
   (d) **National Information Centre for Drug and Pharmaceutical**.

9. ERIC databases in USA covers the information regarding
   (a) **education** (b) energy
   (c) environment (d) mathematics.
10. NISSAT's sectoral information centre on drug is located at
   (a) Pune (b) **Lucknow**
   (c) New Delhi (d) Chennai.
11. The Library and Information Division of ICAR is the national centre for all
   (a) INIS activities (b) **AGRIS activities**
   (c) FAO activities (d) UNISIST activities.
12. NISSAT is responsible for rendering of information services in the field of
   (a) research and development
   (b) **science and technology**
   (c) agriculture
   (d) medicine.
13. INIS stands for
   (a) Indian Naval Information System
   (b) Indian Narcotics Information Service
   (c) **International Nuclear Information System**
   (d) Indian National Information System.
14. BLAISE is operating in
   (a) Canada (b) **U. K.**
   (c) U. S. A. (d) India.
15. The library and information and information services division of BARC is the national centre for
   (a) all UNISIST activities in India
   (b) all FAO activities in India
   (c) **all INIS activities in India**
   (d) all IFLA activities in India.
16. Grey literature means
   (a) external reports published as documents
   (b) **internal reports not published as documents**
   (c) external reports not published as documents

(d) internal reports published as documents.

17. The currently used full form of OCLC is
 (a) Ohio College Library Center
 (b) **Online Computer Library Center**
 (c) Online Catalogue of Library of Congress
 (d) none of these.
18. UBC stands for
 (a) **Universal Bibliographic Control**
 (b) Universal Bibliographic Classification
 (c) United Bibliographic Control
 (d) none of these.
19. RLIN is an information network functioning in
 (a) UK (b) Canada
 (c) Germany (d) **USA**.
20. The UAP stands for
 (a) Universal Advance Programmeming
 (b) Universal Academic Problems
 (c) Universal Academic Publication
 (d) **Universal Availability of Publication**.
21. A system contains
 (a) **interrelated parts having a purpose**
 (b) unrelated parts
 (c) unrelated parts having different purpose
 (d) none of these.
22. INIS is an example of
 (a) distributed input and centralised output
 (b) centralised input and output
 (c) **centralised input and distributed output**
 (d) distributed input and output.
23. Which of the following network is not primarily for academic purposes?
 (a) ERNET (b) JANET
 (c) **NICNET** (d) INFLIBNET.
24. Transboarder data flow means
 (a) exchange of documents between countries

(b) free flow of books between countries
(c) **exchange of electronic information between countries**
(d) none of these.

25. UAP is a programme of
(a) UNESCO (b) **IFLA**
(c) FID (d) British Library.

26. INFLIBNET is a programme sponsored by
(a) NISSAT
(b) Planning Commission
(c) Ministry of Electronics
(d) **UGC**.

27. The World Cat Service is provided by
(a) RLIN (b) **OCLC**
(c) LC (d) WLN.

28. Which is the World's largest and most comprehensive bibliographic database?
(a) First search (b) OCLC Access Service
(c) **World Cat** (d) Prompt Cat.

29. The Universal Bibliographic Control (UBC) programme (1974) was sponsored by
(a) FID (b) UNESCO
(c) **IFLA** (d) LC.

30. Information is a trinity consisting of content, conduit, and
(a) value (b) resource
(c) **context** (d) power.

31. The information services provided by utilizing telecommunication technology may be categorized in
(a) two broad groups (b) **three broad groups**
(c) four broad groups (d) five broad categories.

32. Development Information System is maintained by
(a) **UNESCO** (b) UN
(c) INSDOC (d) UGC.

INFORMATION RETRIEVAL SERVICES

1. The name of S. C. Bradford is associated with
   (a) occurrence of terms in a paragraph
   (b) number of articles written by an author
   (c) **law of scattering**
   (d) citation of an article.
2. 'Recall' and 'Precision' are the terms used in
   (a) reference service
   (b) **information retrieval system**
   (c) library management
   (d) book selection.
3. PRECIS has been developed by
   (a) E. J. Coates (b) **Derek Austin**
   (c) S. R. Ranganathan (d) Mortimer Taube.
4. POPSI is a
   (a) post co-ordinate indexing system
   (b) keyword based indexing system
   (c) **pre co-ordinate indexing system**
   (d) citation indexing.
5. Controlled vocabulary in indexing is called
   (a) **a thesaurus**
   (b) a language dictionary
   (c) a dictionary of synonyms
   (d) a list of subject headings.
6. The concept of 'Paperless Society' was first given by
   (a) Derek Austin (b) **F. W. Lancaster**
   (c) Jesse H. Shera (d) Maurice F. Taube.
7. The term 'Information Retrieval' was coined by
   (a) B. C. Vickery (b) S. R. Ranganathan
   (c) F. W. Lancaster (d) **Calvin N. Mooers**.
8. The effect of reduction in the level of specificity of indexing on information retrieval is that it
   (a) increases precision and decreases recall
   (b) **increases recall and decreases precision**

(c) increases recall and precision both

(d) decreases recall and precision both.

9. The process of retrieving detail / document relevant to a query from a catalogue/ database adequately defines

(a) documentation

(b) acquisition

(c) **information retrieval services**

(d) cataloguing services.

10. The term 'recall' is used in information retrieval to refer to

(a) recollect the documents

(b) **the ability of a system to retrieve relevant documents**

(c) to recollect the irrelevant documents

(d) to retrieve irrelevant documents.

11. 'Truncation' is a technique used in

(a) cataloguing

(b) classification

(c) reference service

(d) **online information retrieval**.

12. The logic 'And', 'Or', and 'Not' was devised by

(a) F. W. Lancaster (b) **George Boole**

(c) S. R. Ranganathan (d) M. A. Gopinath.

13. Lotka's law is concerned with

(a) single number of paper per author

(b) two papers per author

(c) three papers per author

(d) **average number of papers per author**.

14. The mathematical theory of communication is associated with

(a) S. Ramanujan (b) S. R. Ranganathan

(c) I. N. Sengupta (d) **Shannon and Weaver**.

15. 'Bibliometrics' is a study of

(a) **quantitative analysis of publications**

(b) qualitative analysis of publications

(c) macro analysis of publications

(d) micro analysis of publications.

16. The Shanon –Weaver Model of Information as criticized for

(a) being too mathematical

(b) being unidirectional

(c) being primarily suited to electronic commission

(d) **all of the above**.

17. There are a total number of 50 relevant documents in a collection response to a query, only 30 documents are retrieved of these only 10 were relevant. What is the recall percentage?

(a) 20% (b) **33%**

(c) 40% (d) 60%.

18. The concept of 'Librametry' was developed by

(a) S. C. Bradford (b) J. D. Bernal

(c) D. J. Foskett (d) **S. R. Ranganathan**.

19. A retrieval system retrieves a total of 50 documents. Out of these 40 are irrelevant. Another 10 documents which were relevant but not retrieved. The precision percentage for that query would be

(a) 40% (b) **20%**

(c) 60% (d) 80%.

20. The query on "Use of Audio Visual Aids in teaching Science at Primary Schools" can be framed as

(a) **Audio Visual aids and Science and Primary Schools**

(b) Audio Visual aids or Science or Primary Schools

(c) Audio Visual aids or Science and Primary schools

(d) Audio Visual aids and Science or Primary Schools.

21. Which of the following can be considered as formal channels of communication?

(a) **Conferences, Research Reports, Theses**

(b) Research Reports, Correspondence, Books

(c) Short Communication, Journals, E-Mail, Theses

(d) Conversations, Electronic Journals, Research Reports.

22. A device for searching through a fragment of the search term so that it can match related terms starting with the same term is known as
(a) Boolean Search (b) **Truncation**
(c) Thesaurus (d) Indexing Language.

23. Venn diagram was developed by
(a) **John Venn** (b) Peter Venn
(c) Alfred Venn (d) Marlos Venn.

24. The merit of what type of searching is to offer the using of Boolean logic which allows limiting or expanding the search, as required?
(a) manual searching (b) **online searching**
(c) literature searching (d) reference searching.

COMPUTER APPLICATION IN LIBRARIES

1. CD-ROM is a
(a) computer language (b) **storage device**
(c) application software (d) operating system.

2. PC falls in the category of
(a) super computer (b) mainframe computer
(c) mini computer (d) **micro computer**.

3. LAN stands for
(a) Library Automation Network
(b) Library and Network
(c) Library Area Network
(d) **Local Area Network**.

4. VDUs in computers are used for
(a) input (b) **output**
(c) control (d) storage.

5. UNIX is
(a) computer hardware
(b) application software
(c) computer high level language
(d) **operating system**.

6. The IT used for simulation of the human thought is known as
   (a) thinking simulation
   (b) third generation computers
   (c) thought process mechanism
   (d) **artificial intelligence**.
7. RAM stands for
   (a) Read Access Memory
   (b) Read and Memory
   (c) Read Active Memory
   (d) **Random Access Memory**.
8. CDS/ISIS is a
   (a) computer language
   (b) part of computer hardware
   (c) **software package**
   (d) none of these.
9. The example of programmeming language is
   (a) CPU (b) VDU
   (c) Hard Drive (d) **Pascal**.
10. Arithmetic and Logical Unit in the context of computer denotes
   (a) software (b) **hardware**
   (c) programmeming unit (d) printing unit.
11. Modem is a
   (a) software device
   (b) scanner
   (c) CD drive
   (d) **hardware device that converts from one form to another**.
12. The example of a high level language is
   (a) adobe photo shop (b) Auto CAD
   (c) macromedia flash (d) **ForTran**.
13. CD-ROM stands for
   (a) Compact Disk Read Output Memory
   (b) Compact disk Read On Memory

(c) Compact Disk Read Over Memory
(d) **Compact Disk Read Only Memory**.

14. The memory part of computer's CPU is also known as
(a) external storage unit (b) **internal storage unit**
(c) data storage unit (d) language storage unit.

15. CDS/ISIS package has been developed by
(a) UNISIST (b) **UNESCO**
(c) IFLA (d) FAO.

16. Basic is a
(a) hardware item
(b) part of Internet communication
(c) **programmeming language**
(d) none of these.

17. Valves and tubes were used as main processors in
(a) **1st generation computers**
(b) 2nd generation computers
(c) 3rd generation computers
(d) 4th generation computers.

18. MINISIS requires for its operation
(a) Pentium1 computer system
(b) Pentium2 computer system
(c) 486 computer system
(d) **HP3000 computer system**.

19. Volatile memory is referred to as
(a) ROM (b) EPROM
(c) **RAM** (d) none of these.

20. In the context of computers 'BIT' stands for
(a) Binary Information Technology
(b) Booting Information Technology
(c) Binary Input Technology
(d) **Binary Digit**.

21. Computerised library house keeping is done with
(a) system software (b) **application software**
(c) CPU (d) VDU.

22. DBase is a

(a) **application software** (b) system software
(c) internal storage (d) external storage.

23. In WordStar for opening a file the option given is
(a) A (b) B
(c) C (d) **D**.

24. In computer terminology 'C' refers to
(a) **programmeming language**
(b) cabinet
(c) cache memory
(d) COBOL.

25. CDS/ISIS is operated through
(a) Unix (b) Linux
(c) **DOS** (d) Windows.

26. In CDS/ISIS for creating a new record the option given is
(a) L (b) M
(c) **N** (d) P.

27. IBM stands for
(a) International Binary Machines
(b) International Booting Machines
(c) **International Business Machines, Inc.**
(d) none of these.

28. Byte refers to
(a) a string of five binary digits
(b) a sting of six binary digits
(c) a string of seven binary digits
(d) **a string of eight binary digits**.

29. The following are the useful input devices
(a) Keyboard, RAM and CD-ROMs
(b) **OCR, Light Pens and Keyboards**
(c) CD-ROM, OCR and Floppy Disks
(d) Hard Disks, Magnetic Tapes and Light Pens.

30. Which of the following is not a computer programmeming language?
(a) FORTRAN (b) Basic

(c) **COBOL** (d) ASCII.

31. In the binary system of numbers 100 represents the decimal number
    (a) 100 (b) 1
    (c) **4** (d) 3.
32. In relation to computer Basic is
    (a) core memory (b) hardware
    (c) model (d) **language**.
33. Arrange the following storage devices according to increasing capacity (a) magnetic tapes; (b) CD-ROMs; (c) Floppy disks; (d) Magnetic disks.
    (a) **(c), (a), (d), (b)** (b) (a), (b), (c), (d)
    (c) (d), (c), (a), (b) (d) (d), (a), (b), (c).
34. The following software is a typical example of an operating system
    (a) **DOS** (b) WordStar
    (c) dBase III+ (d) Lotus 1-2-3.
35. Computers are used for handling large mass of
    (a) **information and its quick retrieval**
    (b) books and its quick retrieval
    (c) news and its quick retrieval
    (d) libraries and its quick retrieval.

LIBRARY ADMINISTRATION AND MANAGEMENT

1. PERT is a technique for
   (a) collection of data (b) job analysis
   (c) **system analysis** (d) job description.
2. 'Staff manual' is a record which gives information about
   (a) periodicals
   (b) abstracting
   (c) indexing
   (d) **modifications introduced in classification and cataloguing procedures**.

3. Organizational charts show the structure of an organization in the way
   (a) horizontal
   (b) vertical
   (c) **horizontal and vertical**
   (d) diagonal.
4. The methods of estimating funds for libraries are propotional method of details and
   (a) per member
   (b) **per capita**
   (c) total users
   (d) total users and estimated non-users.
5. The number of principles of management identified by H. Fayol was
   (a) sixteen (b) fifteen
   (c) **fourteen** (d) thirteen.
6. PODSCORB was developed by
   (a) F. W. Taylor (b) H. Fayol
   (c) B. C. Vickery (d) **Gulick and Urwick**.
7. The slogan 'Best books in the largest number at the least cost' said
   (a) F. Drury (b) **Melvil Dewey**
   (c) F. W. Lancaster (d) S. R. Ranganathan.
8. Authority file is used in
   (a) periodical division
   (b) classification and cataloguing division
   (c) **technical division**
   (d) referral service division.
9. Cost benefit analysis means
   (a) **performance evaluation based on cost**
   (b) performance evaluation based on benefit
   (c) performance evaluation based on opening cost
   (d) performance evaluation based on closing cost.
10. H. Fayol belonged to
   (a) scientific school of management
   (b) **classical school of management**

(c) Scientific and classical school of management
(d) none of the above.

11. For acquisition of 6000 books in a library in a year, Dr. S. R. Ranganathan in his staff formula has recommended
(a) two professional staff (b) three professional staff
(c) four professional staff (d) **one professional staff.**

12. Preparation of library budget without considering previous year's budget is known as
(a) master budget (b) **zero base budget**
(c) cash budget (d) financial budget.

13. Organization structure is the
(a) **blue print of structure of an organization**
(b) blue print of structure of management
(c) blue print of structure of co-ordination
(d) blue print of structure of control.

14. The description of relation between work and time by using the charts is known as
(a) organization chart (b) flow chart
(c) **Gantt chart** (d) bar chart.

15. The process of analysing a given job into different distinct items is known as
(a) job chart (b) **job analysis**
(c) job allotment (d) job enrichment.

16. The fastest charging system is
(a) Newark system (b) **Brown system**
(c) ledger system (d) dummy system.

17. PPBS relates to
(a) reference service (b) referral service
(c) circulation service (d) **budget.**

18. The management approach which holds that the group co-ordination and effective behaviour automatically emerge around a group natural leader is known as
(a) scientific approach (b) **spontaneity approach**
(c) casual approach (d) modern approach.

19. 'Living with Books' deals with library

(a) book accessioning (b) book cataloguing
(c) book classification (d) **book selection**.

20. Zero base budgeting means
(a) There will be no increase in expenses or income
(b) **There will be no budget**
(c) The difference between income and expenditure is zero
(d) All proposals for income and expenditure will need to be justified

21. If a new library wants to provide for 10000 books how many catalogue trays should it plan for?
(a) **10** (b) 40
(c) 80 (d) 100.

22. The method of budgeting which is not concerned with what happened previously but is more concerned with the requirements of the future, is known as
(a) Line budget (b) Programme budget
(c) Formula budget (d) **Zero base budget**.

23. The Brown charging system will not show
(a) when a particular book is to be returned
(b) **which book had been borrowed earlier by a member**
(c) the number of books over due
(d) the number of books issued in a subject.

24. Shelf list cards
(i) replicate the arrangement of the shelves
(ii) are used in stock verification
(iii) represent each volume on the staff.
Which of the phrases is correct?
a) **i) &(ii)** (b) (i) & (iii)
c) (ii) & (iii) (d) all.

25. The standard width of a library rack is
(a) $2^{1/2'}$ (b) **3'**
(c) $3^{1/2'}$ (d) 4'

26. Span of control refers to
(a) **the number of subordinates to be supervised**

(b) exercise the strict control over the staff
(c) duration over which the control is to be exercised
(d) the area which is to be controlled.

27. If a new library wants to provide for 10,000 books how many double sided standard size racks are needs
(a) **20** (b) 100
(c) 10 (d) 50.

28. "The library will subscribe two journals through an agent". This is a statement of
(a) objective (b) policy
(c) **procedure** (d) mission.

29. "Remainders" are
(a) funds left over after purchasing books
(b) **books which are not bought last year**
(c) the space is divided into equal units
(d) different units are built for different functions.

30. Which person in the following is not associated with theories of motivation?
(a) Maslow (b) Herzberg McGregor
(d) **Hawthorne**.

31. Functional element of management is known as
(a) PSODCORB (b) **POSDCORB**
(c) POSBCORB (d) POSDCROB.

32. Modular planning of library building means
(a) the library is built in stages
(b) models are built before the final building
(c) **the space is divided into equal units**
(d) different units are built for different functions.

33. A library has the following sections: Children's section, Periodical section, Audio-Visual section and Braille section, which of the following criteria have been used for departmentalisation?
(a) **Function and Customer**
(b) Customer and Product
(c) Function and Product
(d) Function, Product and Customer.

34. GOC stands for
    (a) Government Office Control
    (b) General Office Control
    (c) **Good Offices Committee**
    (d) Good Office Conduct.
35. Kardex system is adopted in libraries for
    (a) maintenance of news clipping
    (b) **maintenance of records of periodicals subscription**
    (c) filling of microforms
    (d) cataloguing of books.
36. Modern management is characterised by a
    (a) logistic approach
    (b) **scientific approach**
    (c) hypothetical approach
    (d) psychological approach.
37. System approach enriches what to achieve a common goal?
    (a) attitude of the staff
    (b) work environment
    (c) financial position
    (d) **management functions**.
38. Which function involves analysing the entire activities of an organization into homogeneous types of works and jobs?
    (a) Reporting (b) **Organising**
    (c) planning (d) Centralisation.
39. "Unity is Strength" is the principle of management advocated by
    (a) Barnard (b) **Fayol**
    (c) Taylor (d) S. R. Rangathan.
40. Staffing is concerned with providing and maintaining
    (a) financial resources (b) **human resources**
    (c) technical resources (d) physical resources.
41. Which function improves the planning and control of operations by providing better information for decision making?

(a) System Analysis
(b) Operation Management
(c) **Management Information System**
(d) Monitoring Technique.

42. Book selection committee comes under the category of
(a) Statutory Committee (b) Standing Committee
(c) Adhoc Committee (d) **Working Committee**.

43. Government documents are generally divided into two categories such as
(a) **published and unpublished**
(b) parliamentary and non-parliamentary
(c) conventional and neo-conventional
(d) primary and secondary.

44. "Right book to the right reader at the right time" should be the principle of book selection enunciated by
(a) **Drury** (b) Melvil Dewey
(c) McColvin (d) john Otlet.

45. What is the central character in Drury's principle of book selection?
(a) staff (b) **reader**
(c) library collection (d) building.

46. MBO stands for
(a) **Management By Objectives**
(b) Maintenance By Objectives
(c) Management Based objectives
(d) Managed By Objectives.

47. Acquisition work in a library comprises three distinct functions selection, procurement and
(a) computerisation (b) **accessioning**
(c) issue (d) return.

48. Micro images printed on a sheet or film is called
(a) **microfilm** (b) opaque card
(c) microfiche (d) patent.

49. Newly acquired books are entered in
(a) Stock Register
(b) Log Book Register

(c) **Accession Register**
(d) Circulation Sheet Register.

50. What percentage of trade discount is usually admissible on books?
(a) 25% (b) 30%
(c) 20% (d) **10%**.

51. Conversation rates create problems while buying
(a) **foreign periodicals**
(b) govt. documents
(c) conference proceedings
(d) reference collection.

52. Which institution decides conversion rates of foreign currencies and discount applicable to Indian libraries while purchasing books and periodicals?
(a) NIC (b) GILA
(c) ILA (d) **GOC**.

53. Requesting a borrower to return the book before its due date is called
(a) holds (b) reserve
(c) **recall** (d) lending.

54. A page chosen and uniformly used in all documents for writing accession number is know as
(a) recto (b) clue page
(c) secret page (d) **verso**.

55. Procurement of foreign periodicals are done through Direct Subscription and
(a) Personal Correspondence
(b) Government
(c) Embassy
(d) **Agency Method**

56. Which document shows the decisions taken on practices of the library relating to classification and cataloguing?
(a) **Authority File** (b) Work Diary
(c) Shelf List (d) Catalogue Cards.

57. A user who seeks extension of time for borrowed books is known as
(a) issue (b) reminder
(c) **renewal** (d) lending.

58. Back issues of periodicals and magazines require
(a) leather binding (b) **half leather binding**
(c) full leather binding (d) cloth binding.

59. Sheets before and after the text of a book are called
(a) **endpapers** (b) collation
(c) gilding (d) head bands.

60. According to ALA standards for class A binding, which board is a medium quality board as well as it is compact and hard wearing?
(a) **grey** (b) split
(c) mill (d) straw.

61. Which is better than cure?
(a) Preservation (b) Conservation
(c) Reservation (d) **Prevention**.

62. Human Resources Development is a process which aims at improving of the employees of an organization in respect of
(a) personality (b) **skills and competence**
(c) social obligation (d) technological skills.

63. The process of introducing new entrants into the organization is called
(a) selection (b) induction
(c) deployment (d) **orientation.**

64. Who can make or manage the institution?
(a) **authority** (b) finance
(c) personnel (d) politics.

65. Which technique allows its employees, individuals or groups to take part in decision making?
(a) Operation Management
(b) Personnel Management
(c) Leadership
(d) **Participative Management**.

66. Which approach gives emphasis on customers needs or expectations?
    (a) MIS (b) **TQM**
    (c) DSS (d) CPM.
67. One of the guiding principles of financial management is
    (a) adequate spending (b) irregularity in spending
    (c) rigidity in expenditure (d) **effective control**.
68. Which method takes into account the actual amount of expenditure spent on each item?
    (a) **Proportional Method** (b) Method of Details
    (c) Percapita Method (d) Programme Method.
69. Which budgeting does not take into account of what happened in the past but places emphasis on the current activities?
    (a) Programme budgeting (b) Performance budgeting
    (c) **Zero-base budgeting** (d) Centralised budgeting.
70. Systematic maintenance of the income and expenditure flow on records called as
    (a) Auditing (b) Accounting
    (c) **Budgeting** (d) Reporting.
71. The main purpose of library accounting is to keep expenditures within the
    (a) **budget** (b) cash book
    (c) plan expenditure (d) non-plan expenditure.
72. The daily income and expenditure of an institution is entered in
    (a) Ledger (b) **Cash Book**
    (c) Bill Register (d) Book of Drawl.

LIBRARY AND SOCIETY

1. The state which does not provide for library cess is
   (a) Tamil Nadu (b) Andhra Pradesh
   (c) **West Bengal** (d) Karnataka.
2. Parry Committee Report (UK) relates to
   (a) Public Libraries (b) **University Libraries**
   (c) National Libraries (d) Special Libraries.
3. The ILA was founded in the year
   (a) 1924 (b) **1933**
   (c) 1950 (d) 1952.
4. The state that enacted library legislation in 1965 is
   (a) **Karnataka** (b) Haryana
   (c) Goa (d) Manipur.
5. William A. Borden, the first librarian in Baroda state, came from
   (a) UK (b) **USA**
   (c) France (d) Australia.
6. Library of Congress is
   (a) **National Library of the USA**
   (b) The Library of Indian Congress
   (c) The Library of the Parliament of India
   (d) National Library of Australia
7. 'Libri' is published from
   (a) **Denmark** (b) U. K.
   (c) U. S. A. (d) Australia
8. 'Library Literature' is published by
   (a) DESIDOC (b) **H. W. Wilson**
   (c) INSDOC (d) R. C. Bowker.
9. Science Information Centre of the UGC is located at
   (a) INSDOC
   (b) **Indian Institute of Science, Bangalore**
   (c) DESIDOC
   (d) DRTC.
10. The centre which is not a Sectoral Information Centre of NISSAT is

(a) Central Food Technological Research Institute (Mysore)
(b) Central Drug Research Institute (Lucknow)
(c) Central Machine Tools Institute (Bangalore)
(d) **Central Road Research Institute (New Delhi)**.

11. The Headquarters of INFLIBNET is located at
(a) Delhi (b) Mumbai
(c) Bangalore (d) **Ahmedabad**.

12. UNISIST is
(a) **World Science Information Programme**
(b) documentation centre in the US
(c) type of special information service in science & technology
(d) an indexing system.

13. INIS stands for
(a) **Information Network in Nuclear Science & Technology**
(b) Library Development Programme in Nuclear Science
(c) Information Network in Naval Science
(d) Information Network in Information Science.

14. 'Right book to the right reader at right time' is a principle enumerated by
(a) Ranganathan (b) Dewey
(c) **Drury** (d) Haines.

15. The professional organization concerned mainly with teachers of library science in India is
(a) IASLIC (b) ILA
(c) BLA (d) **IATLIS**.

16. Andrew Carnegie was concerned with
(a) Library and Information Science
(b) Information Technology
(c) Mathematics
(d) **Philanthrophy**.

17. Kenyan Committee of UK was concerned with
(a) school libraries (b) university libraries

(c) research libraries (d) **public libraries**.

18. Obligation of state to provide library services to masses is related with
(a) 1st law of Library Science
(b) **2nd law of Library Science**
(c) 3rd law of Library science
(d) 4th law of Library Science.

19. 'Manifesto for Public Libraries' was published by
(a) IFLA (b) UNISIST
(c) **UNESCO** (d) ALA.

20. The first Library Science school was started by Melvil Dewey in
(a) Yale University (b) Chicago University
(c) Harvard University (d) **Columbia University**.

21. The first act of Parliament to provide free public library service was passed in Great Britain in
(a) 1860 (b) 1834
(c) **1850** (d) 1856.

22. General Information Programme (PGI) is connected with
(a) ALA (b) IFLA
(c) ILA (d) **UNESCO**.

23. 'Child growth' and 'adult growth' has been discussed by S. R. Ranganathan is concerned with
(a) 2nd law of Library Science
(b) 3rd law of Library Science
(c) 4th law of Library Science
(d) **5th law of Library Science**.

24. The Library Association (Great Britain) was founded in
(a) 1876 (b) 1878
(c) **1877** (d) 1879.

25. Library extension activity is not related with
(a) mobile library service
(b) book fair and exhibition
(c) lecture on library matters
(d) **inter library loan**.

26. IFLA was founded in the year
    (a) 1937 (b) **1927**
    (b) 1928 (d) 1929.
27. British Library is a
    (a) University Library (b) Research Llibrary
    (c) College Library (d) **National Library**.
28. The Advisory Committee for libraries appointed by the Government of India is also known as
    (a) Chattopadhyay Committee
    (b) **Sinha Committee**
    (c) Ranganathan Committee
    (d) Parry Committee.
29. The first librarian of National Library was
    (a) M. A. Gopinath (b) I. K. Ravichandra Rao
    (c) S. R. Ranganathan (d) **B. S. Kesavan.**
30. The Library Legislation was not passed in the state of
    (a) West Bengal (b) Orissa
    (c) Andhra Pradesh (d) **Punjab.**
31. The third law of Library Science is
    (a) every reader his/her book
    (b) **every book its reader**
    (c) books are for use
    (d) save the time of the user.
32. The first university which offered Ph. D. in Library Science in India is
    (a) Madras University (b) Jadavpur University
    (c) Punjab University (d) **Delhi University**.
33. The person associated with library movement in India is
    (a) F. W. Lancaster (b) Blaise Cronin
    (c) **W. A. Borden** (d) Thomas Childers.
34. The person associated with library movement in the erstwhile state of Baroda
    (a) Balaji Baji Rao (b) Shibaji
    (c) Shambhaji Rao
    (d) **Maharaja Sayaji Rao Gaikward**.

35. UNESCO came into existence in the year

(a) 1947 (b) 1956

(c) **1946** (d) 1948.

36. The particular law of Library Science makes it obligatory on the part of the state to enact library legislation is

(a) 1st law of Library Science

(b) 3rd law of Library Science

(c) 4th law of Library Science

(d) **2nd law of Library Science**.

37. The year was declared as international year of literacy in

(a) 1992 (b) 1991

(c) **1990** (d) 1993.

38. Mobile library service is mainly a tool for

(a) inter-library loan (b) reference service

(c) referral service (d) **library extension** work.

39. In the enactment of the British Public Library Act of 1850, a major played by

(a) Edward Robinson (b) **Edward Edwards**

(c) Edward Marshall (d) Edward Samuelson.

40. The present name of ASLIB is

(a) Association of Library and Information Bureaux

(b) Association of Special Library and Information Bureaux

(c) Association of Special Information Bureaux

(d) **Association for Information Management**.

41. The first librarian of Imperial Library was

(a) John McDonald (b) John Maxmuller

(c) John Abraham (d) **John McFarlane**.

42. Indian Library Association takes into its fold to

(a) public libraries (b) university libraries

(c) research libraries (d) **all types of libraries**.

43. The state does not have a Public Libraries Act

(a) **Gujarat** (b) Kerala

(c) Mizoram (d) Delhi.

44. ALA was established in
    (a) 1880 (b) 1881
    (c) 1882 (d) **1876**.
45. The National Library, Calcutta Act came into force in
    (a) 1949 (b) 1950
    (c) **1952** (d) 1951.
46. First Master's degree programme in Library Science in India was started by
    (a) Jawaharlal Nehru University
    (b) **The University of Delhi**
    (c) Madras University
    (d) Gulberga University.
47. The number of Indian states has passed library legislation up to 2003
    (a) 10 (b) 11
    (c) **12** (d) 13.
48. Delhi Public Library was established in the year
    (a) 1955 (b) 1957
    (c) **1950** (d) 1960.
49. The IFLA Annual General Conference, 1992 was held in
    (a) London (b) Paris
    (c) New York (d) **India**
50. Library Week in India is organised during the month of
    (a) September (b) October
    (c) **November** (d) December.
51. Library movement in the erstwhile state of Baroda started in the year
    (a) 1911 (b) 1912
    (c) **1910** (d) 1913.
52. Ranganathan Committee Report on development of university and college libraries was published by
    (a) DESIDOC (b) DRTC
    (c) **UGC** (d) ILA.
53. The latest library act was passed by

(a) Mizoram (b) Kerala
(c) Goa (d) **Orissa**.

54. The activity does not fall under purview of library extension
(a) mobile library service
(b) book fair
(c) exhibition on library matters
(d) **extending the library building**.

55. According to Education Commission, 1964-66, the percentage of university budget should be earmarked for its library expenditure is
(a) 5.5% (b) 7.5%
(c) **6.5%** (d) 8.5%.

56. The headquarters of IFLA is located at
(a) Paris (b) Sweden
(c) Chicago (d) **The Hague**.

57. Second library school was started in
(a) Kakatiya University (b) Bundelkhand University
(c) Osmania Unversity (d) **Punjab University**.

58. First library training school was started in
(a) Hyderabad University
(b) The University of Calcutta
(c) Anna University
(d) **Madras University**.

59. Which committee/commission described Public Libraries as 'Stagnating Pools of Books'?
(a) Ranganathan Committee
(b) Sinha Committee
(c) **Fyzee Committee**
(d) Kothari Committee.

60. A Professional Association should primarily
(a) function as a trade union
(b) **work for the development of its members**
(c) undertake research in professional techniques
(d) serve as an employment exchange.

61. Extension services to the blinds by the public library is justified by
    (a) the second law of Library Science
    (b) the fifth law of Library Science
    (c) the first law of Library Science
    (d) **all of the above**.

62. The National Library, Kolkata receives books on deposit under
    (a) The Registration of Books Act, 1887
    (b) **The Delivery of Books Act, 1954**
    (c) The Copyright Act, 1935
    (d) all of the above.

63. Library Legislation supports the Public Library Movement by
    (a) **ensuring that funds are made available**
    (b) establishing local library authorities
    (c) making library services mandatory
    (d) all of the above.

64. Library orientation, bibliographic instruction and user education are related in the following way
    (a) all mean the same thing
    (b) **user education is wider and encompasses the other two**
    (c) library orientation is wider and encompasses the other two
    (d) none of these.

66. Which of the following should be the primary objective of a college library?
    (a) to promote research activities
    (b) to encourage reading habits
    (c) **to support teaching programmes of the college**
    (d) to provide for the recreational needs of the students.

67. Zero growth libraries that
    (a) libraries must not buy books
    (b) libraries do not get more space

(c) libraries must need but many books as they aid

(d) **libraries do not get more funds**.

68. With which agency did UNESCO collaborate to establish UNISIST?

(a) **ICSU** (b) FID

(c) IFLA (d) ALA.

69. The Raja Rammohan Roy Library Foundation was established in the year

(a) **1972** (b) 1973

(c) 1977 (d) 1987.

70. Public libraries support which type of education?

(a) formal (b) vocational

(c) **non-formal** (d) technical.

71. In which society Information and knowledge are considered as principal resources?

(a) agricultural society (b) **information society**

(c) eastern society (d) industrial society.

72. The laws of Library Science contribute to good librarianship enunciated by

(a) Melvil Dewey

(b) American Library Association

(c) Prof. B. S. Kesavan

(d) **Dr. S. R. Ranganathan**.

73. The first law of Library science has implication on which location of library?

(a) stack

(b) **building**

(c) furniture and equipment

(d) records and registers.

74. The third law of Library Science works in full conformity with

(a) resource sharing (b) closed access

(c) obligation of staff (d) **open access**.

75. "Library is a growing organism" means library grows by the number of books, readers and

(a) audio visuals (b) computers

(c) **staff** (d) budget.

76. While planning and designing a library building there should be adequate provision of expansion both horizontally and

(a) breadth (b) **vertically**

(c) length (d) radius.

77. Which Report made a number of recommendations for the development of public libraries?

(a) J. S. Mill

(b) **McColvin**

(c) Prof. S. Radha Krishnan

(d) Melvil Dewey.

78. Mercantile libraries were established to foster educational and recreational reading among their employees in

(a) **USA** (b) France

(c) India (d) U. K.

79. Deptt. Of Culture, Govt. of India took initiative for the development of libraries in the country through a draft document namely

(a) National Education Policy (b) **NAPLIS**

(c) National Information Policy (d) IASLIC.

80. The National Library, Kolkata was earlier known as

(a) **The Imperial Library**

(b) The Asiatic Society Library

(c) The National Public Library

(d) Connemera Public Library.

81. The biggest library in the world is

(a) Delhi Public Library

(b) **The Library of Congress**

(c) The British Library

(d) National Library, Kolkata.

82. For maintenance and development of the library, Prof. K. N. Raj Committee recommended

(a) 10% (b) 25%

(c) **20%** (d) 15%.

83. Which of the following state first enacted Public Libraries Act?
(a) Gujrat (b) **Tamil Nadu**
(c) Andhra Pradesh (d) West Bengal.

84. One of the important functions of a national library is preparation of
(a) Union Catalogue
(b) National Catalogue
(c) **National Bibliography**
(d) National Index.

85. The British Library is responsible for publishing
(a) **British National Bibliography**
(b) UK Public Libraries Act
(c) Books in Print
(d) Wales Bibliography.

86. School, College and University libraries constitute
(a) public libraries (b) **academic libraries**
(c) research libraries (d) special libraries.

87. Which has taken a number of steps to organize and improve the services of school libraries in India?
(a) **NCERT** (b) KVS
(c) CBSE (d) ILA.

88. In 1994, UNESCO published a Manifesto dealing with
(a) Medical libraries (b) **Public libraries**
(c) Agricultural libraries (d) College libraries.

89. Which of the following state enacted Public Libraries Act in 1989?
(a) Andhra Pradesh (b) Gujrat
(c) **Haryana** (d) Goa.

90. Mizoram Public Libraries Act was enacted in the year of
(a) **1993** (b) 1990
(c) 1978 (d) 1991.

91. The state central library of Tamil Nadu is
(a) Madras University Library
(b) **Connemara Public Library**

(c) Ranganathan's Public Library
(d) IIT Library.

92. Which Public Libraries Act provides reservation of woman and one ST members to all Library Committees?
(a) Goa (b) West Bengal
(c) **Kerala** (d) Mizoram.

93. Which of the following state does not have the provision of library cess?
(a) Tamil Nadu (b) **West Bengal**
(c) Karnataka (d) Andhra Pradesh.

94. Which type of programmes are conducted in order to know the information requirements of the readers?
(a) Orientation Programmes
(b) Workshops
(c) **User Studies**
(d) Training Programmes.

95. Making users acquainted with the library's usage and services is known as
(a) **User Orientation** (b) User Analysis
(c) User Studies (d) Feed back.

96. Which is concerned with providing instructions to the users how to make use of the information resources available in the libraries?
(a) User Orientation (b) **User Education**
(c) Learner Integration (d) Bibliographic Instruction.

97. The information policy objectives of which institution lay stress on user education?
(a) IFLA (b) FID
(c) UNESCO (d) **UNISIST**.

98. In India, which institution was organized a number of seminars and workshops for promotion of user education?
(a) NASSDOC (b) DRTC
(c) **INSDOC** (d) PARLE.

99. At which institution the British Library has established a Centre for Research on User Studies (CRUX)?

(a) University of Leads (b) Oxford College
(c) University of Wales (d) **University of Sheffield**.

100. CALIBNET and DELNET were established with the support of
(a) RRRLF (b) INSDOC
(c) **NISSAT** (d) NISTAD.

101. The Headquarters of FID are located at
(a) Washington (b) Paris
(c) **The Hague** (d) London.

102. In librarianship, building a good image of the library and information profession in society is known as
(a) National Policy (b) **professional ethics**
(c) library rules (d) library economics.

103. ILA has developed a database of libraries called
(a) NALANDA (b) **Granthalaya**
(c) SOUL (d) Suchika.

104. American Library Association has instituted an award for creative professional
achievement in the name of
(a) John Daniel (b) **Melvil Dewey**
(c) J. H. Shera (d) J. S. Mills.

105. Journal of Librarianship is a serial publication of
(a) The Library Association
(b) Indian Library Association
(c) **American Library Association**
(d) Canada Library association.

106. IFLA has developed an internationally acceptable bibliographic record format named as
(a) UNIMARC (b) **CCF**
(c) CANMARC (d) UKMARC.

107. The 49th FID Congress and Conference was held at
(a) London (b) **New Delhi**
(c) Paris (d) Kolkata.

108. UGC provides major financial support to which libraries?

(a) National (b) Public
(c) **University** (d) Technical.

109. UGC Information Centre in Social Sciences is established at
(a) Dr. B. R. Ambedkar University, Lucknow
(b) Utkal University, Bhubaneswar
(c) **Osmania University, Hyderabad**
(d) M. S. University.

110. A national body which provides major financial support to public libraries is
(a) UGC (b) **RRRLF**
(c) NML (d) NBT.

111. INIS is sponsored by
(a) **IAEA** (b) IDRC
(c) FID (d) IFLA.

112. Which institution serves as a national centre for India to AGRIS?
(a) BARC (b) **ARIC**
(c) NIC (d) NISTAD.

113. NISSAT is under the administrative control of
(a) **Dept. of S & T**
(b) DSIR
(c) Deptt. of Education
(d) National Informatics Centre.

114. NISSAT brings out a newsletter namely
(a) IT Bulletin
(b) Information Bulletin
(c) **Information Today and Tomorrow**
(d) Modern IT.

115. Information relating to Defence Studies are provided by
(a) INSDOC (b) **DESIDOC**
(c) NASSDOC (d) NML.

UNIVERSE OF SUBJECTS & RESEARCH METHODOLOGY

1. Inductive logic proceeds from
   (a) general to specific (b) general to general
   (c) **specific to general** (d) specific to specific.
2. Hypothesis is a
   (a) law
   (b) postulate
   (c) canon
   (d) **tentative generalisation**.
3. The scientific method can be applied for research in the field of
   (a) Humanities (b) Natural Sciences
   (c) Social Sciences (d) **all of them**.
4. Research design gives the
   (a) **blue print of the proposed research work**
   (b) blue print of introduction of research
   (c) blue print of conclusion of research
   (d) none of these.
5. First Ph. D. awarded in Library Science by an Indian University was
   (a) S. R. Ranganathan (b) B. S. Kesavan
   (c) M. A. Gopinath (d) **D. B. Krishna Rao**.
6. Solo research is an investigation conducted by
   (a) a team (b) **an individual**
   (c) a department (d) none of these.
7. Historical method of research can be applied
   (a) in History (b) in Social Science
   (c) in Humanities (d) **in all subjects**.
8. Interview is a
   (a) **method of research**
   (b) method of hypothesis
   (c) method of applied research
   (d) method of pure research.

9. First exponent of scientific method was
   (a) Plato (b) Socrates
   (c) Dante (d) **Aristotle**.
10. Correct sequence of cardinal points in the spiral of scientific method is
   (a) Ascendant, Zenith, Descendant, Nadir, Ascendant...
   (b) Zenith, Descendant, Nadir, Ascendant, Zenith...
   (c) Descendant, Nadir, Ascendant, Zenith, Descendant...
   (d) **Nadir, Ascendant, Zenith, Descendant, Nadir...**
11. Research done to find a solution for an immediate problem of the society/industry/business organization is known as
   (a) social research (b) industrial research
   (c) **applied research** (d) pure research.
12. Deductive logic proceeds from
   (a) **general to specific** (b) specific to specific
   (c) specific to general (d) general to general.
13. Nadir, Ascendant, Zenith and Descendant are the four cardinal points of spiral of
   (a) natural science method
   (b) social science method
   (c) **scientific method**
   (d) human science method.
14. The cardinal point which rests at 90^0 from Nadir on the spiral of scientific method is
   (a) **ascendant** (b) zenith
   (c) descendant (d) nadir.
15. In historical method of research, not a tool for collection of data is
   (a) eye witness (b) inscription
   (c) historical evidence (d) **newspaper**.
16. Research aims at immediate results is
   (a) pure research (b) **applied research**
   (c) social research (d) industrial research.

17. One of the cardinal points on the spiral of the scientific method

    (a) natural science (b) social science

    (c) human science (d) **ascendant**.

18. In research on information needs of Chartered Accountants a questionnaire is that to every fifth number of the official register of Chartered Accountants. Would this

    (a) random sampling

    (b) **stratified sampling**

    (c) the whole population

    (d) not a representative sample.

19. In a questionnaire 'open ended' questions are

    (a) **the questions are open to interpretation**

    (b) the answers may be incomplete

    (c) answers may be filled in by respondents

    (d) those where long answers are required.

20. 'Cranfield Studies' are an example of

    (a) survey research (b) **experimental research**

    (c) historical research (d) case study.

21. In a study undertaken to find out how uses approach the library catalogue, all those who use the catalogue on a particular day are interviewed. Would this be considered as?

    (a) **a random sample**

    (b) a stratified sample

    (c) the whole population

    (d) not a representational sample.

22. In a questionnaire, close ended questions are those where:

    (a) the questions and answers are close to each other

    (b) **the answers are given as options**

    (c) the questions are clear and distinct

    (d) short answers are required.

23. A study aimed at finding the best method of shelving library materials

(a) basic research (b) fundamental research
(c) applied research (d) **no research at all**.

24. Formulation of hypothesis is an important component of
(a) content analysis (b) **research design**
(c) processing of data (d) report writing.

25. If you are asked to arrange the concepts "information", "knowledge" and "data" in ascending order of complexity which of the following sequence is correct?
(a) **data – information – knowledge**
(b) knowledge – information – data
(c) information – data –knowledge
(d) information – knowledge – data.

26. Sometimes the terms 'data' and 'knowledge' are synonymously used for
(a) wisdom (b) intelligence
(c) news (d) **information**.

27. A state with its organs of executive, legislature and judiciary, business generates vast amount of
(a) knowledge (b) wisdom
(c) **information** (d) facts.

28. When data is processed, interpreted and presented in an organised form, it becomes
(a) news (b) facts
(c) knowledge (d) **information.**

29. Growth of information beyond a manageable limit characterises the explosion of
(a) books (b) libraries
(c) **information** (d) news.

30. Data on national income presented in a tabular form may be termed as
(a) descriptive information
(b) **statistical information**
(c) enumerative information
(d) societal information.

31. The Metrological Department is responsible for daily collection of
    (a) measurement data (b) income data
    (c) **atmospheric data** (d) demographic data.

32. The forecast note on weather conditions, based on processed and interpreted atmospheric data is
    (a) data (b) news
    (c) facts (d) **information**.

33. The behavioural data of chemical compound under different physical conditions observed through experiment are
    (a) knowledge (b) **raw facts**
    (c) information (d) processed data.

34. The data on national income statistics when reveal the changes that have taken place over a period of time is
    (a) statistical information
    (b) descriptive information
    (c) **analytical information**
    (d) uninterpreted information.

35. Which are the building block of knowledge and all three are handled in libraries offering different types of services?
    (a) Wisdom and information
    (b) **Data and information**
    (c) News and information
    (d) Intelligence and information.

36. Just as, cotton can be loomed into yarns which can be weaved into cloth, data can be weaved into information which can be used to form an organised body of
    (a) **knowledge** (b) information
    (c) wisdom (d) facts.

37. Office of the Registrar General was established to conduct what type of censuses to collect population data?
    (a) **decennial censuses** (b) quarterly censuses
    (c) annual censuses (d) biennial censuses.

38. The progress of a nation is often judged by percentage of national income that is spent on

    (a) education (b) business

    (c) **R&D** (d) surveys.

39. Who enacts various laws?

    (a) Supreme Court (b) High Court

    (c) **Legislatures** (d) Registrar.

40. Who are both consumers and producers of information?

    (a) Teachers (b) Students

    (c) **Researchers** (d) Govt. officials.

41. Large scale use of information in all countries by a wide cross section of people has resulted in coining of terms like

    (a) information explosion

    (b) mass production of information

    (c) **information society**

    (d) information use.

42. Futurologists are specialists in

    (a) **social forecasting** (b) astrology

    (c) astronomy (d) weather forecasting.

43. Quantitative growth of a thing at a particular rate of growth is known as

    (a) periodic growth (b) **exponential growth**

    (c) statistical growth (d) qualitative growth.

Paper II :
OLD TYPE, NET QUESTIONS AND ANSWERS

(December 1998-2000)

(All Answers in Bold Letters)

YEAR WISE ARRANGEMENT

December 1998

1. AACR-II includes rules for
   (a) Bibliographic description and choice of subject heading
   (b) Choice of main entry and subject heading
   (c) Choice of analytical entry and subject heading
   (d) bibliographic description and choice of main and added entries
2. In a classification of persons,the groups – infants, children, adolescents and adults are known as
   (a) A facet (b) A chain
   (c) An array (d) A characteristic
3. In research, inductive logic proceeds from
   (a) Particular to particular
   (b) Particular to general
   (c) General to particular
   (d) General to general
4. One of the main methods of number building using different subject schedule in the DDC is by the
   (a) Relative index (b) Table of auxiliaries
   (c) Add notes (d) None of the above
5. The process of breaking up a specific job into the various tasks involved is
   (a) Job description (b) Job analysis
   (c) Job evaluation (d) Job synthesis
6. Basic research is not concerned with
   (a) Discovering casual relations between facts
   (b) Discovering direct solutions to various practical problems
   (c) Discovering universal laws and theories
   (d) refuting established theories
7. Which of the following is not a secondary source of information
   (a) An encyclopedia (b) An annual review
   (c) A thesis (d) A technical handbook

8. OCR stands for
   (a) Online Computer Retrieval
   (b) Optical Character Recognition
   (c) Online Centre for Reprographics
   (d) Optical Computer Recorder
9. Who among the following is considered as the father of modern management
   (a) Henry Fayol (b) Henry L.Gantt
   (c) Fredrick W. Taylor (d) Fredrick Herzberg
10. Identify the one that does not belong to the group
   (a) MEDLARS **(b) CAS**
   (c) BIOSIS (d) BLAISE
11. Brenda Dervin and M.Kochen have researched on
   (a) Information retrieval
   (b) Information needs
   (c) Computerized library system
   (d) Classification
12. RRRLF is a
   (a) Library association
   (b) A public library
   (c) A public trust for supporting libraries
   (d) A Government body to support public libraries
13. Identify the pair of names responsible for the origin of UDC
   (a) Paul Otlet and Donker Duyvis
   (b) Paul Otlet and Henri La Fontain
   (c) S.C.Bradford and Paul Otlet
   (d) S.C.Bradford and Donker Duyvis
14. A plotter is a
   (a) An input device (b) A memory device
   (c) An output device (d) None of the above
15. NICDRON is situated at
   (a) Calcutta (b) Mumbai
   (c) Chennai **(d) Bangalore**
16. The device that coverts analog signal to digital and vice versa is

(a) MODEM	(b) Analog computer
(b) Digital computer	(d) Digicom

17. Among the following four fundamental categories which category is recognised as 'problem facet"

(a) Personality	(b) Matter
(c) Energy	(d) Space

18. The library will subscribe to journals through an agent. This is a statement of

(a) Objective	**(b) Policy**
(c) Procedure	(d) Mission

19. As per AACR-II, in case of translated works, the translator gets

(a) Main entry	**(b) Added entry**
(c) A Cross reference	(d) Analytical entry

20. The Chairman of the Advisory Committee for Libraries appointed by Government of India in 1957 to investigate the state of libraries in India was

(a) S.R.Ranganathan	**(b) K.P.Sinha**
(c) D.P.Chattopadhyay	(d) A.A.A.Fyzee

21. Among the canons of verbal plane, which canon restrains the use of critical phrases in classification systems

(a) Canon of currency	(b) Canon of context
(b) Canon of reticence	(d) Canon of relevance

22. A bibliography and an index are:

(a) similar, both are locating tools

(b) similar, they are arranged subjectwise

(c) not similar, bibliographies include books, indexes include journal articles

(d) not similar, a bibliography is prepared inhouse, an index is purchased

23. If there is a difference in the title of a book as shown on the title page, half title page, spine, the catalogue should render the title

(a) as on title page

(b) as on the title page, but in square brackets

(c) as on the spine

(d) as on the half title page

24. A survey to determine the reading habits of students is
(a) a descriptive study **(b) an experimental study**
(c) a historical study (d) could be any of the above

June 2000

1. In CC, the principle that helps in the identification of personality category is
(a) cow-calf principle (b) whole-organ principle
(c) Net-neti principle **(d) later-in-time**

2. In DDC Phoenix schedules represent
(a) classes which are slightly modified
(b) classes which are completely changed
(c) classes to be modified in the future
(d) classes not to be modified

3. What is the relationship between ISBD and cataloguing code?
(a) they are not related at all
(b) cataloguing codes will include bibliographic description
(c) ISBD includes cataloguing rules
(d) ISBD can replace cataloguing code

4. Which are of the following is not a part of the MARC record structure?
(a) leader (b) directory
(c) record terminator **(d) check digit**

5. Which of the following combinations is wrong?
(a) PRECIS-Derek Austin-BNB
(b) KWIC-H.P.Luhn-Chemical Titles
(c) Citation Indexing – Eugene Garfield-SCI
(d) Relational Indexing-E.J.Coates-Biological Abstracts

6. Citation indexing was first developed in the field of
(a) Science (b) Mathematics
(c) Law (d) Social Sciences

7. In a thesaurus under a item "internal migration" – which of the following lines would you expect to find
   (a) BT Migration
   (b) NT Rural to Urban Migration
   (c) RT International Migration
   (d) All the above
8. The PERT approach is a device developed to
   (a) better utilize of time in a series of activities
   (b) allow studies to be made between people and machine
   (c) Analyse a workflow to facilitate decision making
   (d) Establish quality control
9. The acronym 'PODSCORB' was coined by
   (a) Gulick and Urwick (b) Taylor
   (c) Mayo (d) Gilberths
10. The basic theory of human motivation was propounded by
   (a) Taylor **(b) Maslow**
   (c) Mayo (d) Likert
11. The method of budgeting, which is not concerned with the requirements of the future is known as
   (a) Line Budget (b) Programme Budget
   (c) Formula Budget **(d) Zero Based Budget**
12. Among the different Boolean operators 'AND' is used
   (a) To widen the search (b) to narrow the search
   (c) to begin the search (d) to end the search
13. Which of the following is not a secondary source of information
   (a) An encyclopedia (b) A text book
   (c) A biographical dictionary **(d) Patents**
14. Which of the following reference source will you consult to locate information on the Pokhran test?
   (a) Encyclopaedia Britannica
   (b) Asian Recorder
   (c) Commonwealth Universities Handbook
   (d) Dictionary of national Biography

15. Information about Indian research studies on bakery and milling is input to IFIS through
    (a) The Central Rice Research Institute
    (b) Indian Agricultural Research Institute
    (c) National Institute of Nutrition
    (d) Central Food Technological Research Institute
16. Which of the following is not an example of Current Awareness Service (CAS)?
    (a) SDI **(b) An Indexing Bulletin**
    (c) Current Contents (d) A Reading List
17. Non-bibliographic Database contain
    (a) Numeric Data (b) Textual Data
    (c) Visual Data **(d) All of the above**
18. Indexing and abstracting sources are available in print, optical and online. Among the three formats there is usually
    (a) a different in price, but not in capability
    (b) no difference in price, but difference in capability
    (c) a difference both in price and in capability
    (d) no difference in price or capability
19. In an empirical study on the impact of television viewing on violence, violence would be
    (a) the dependent variable
    (b) an independent variable
    (c) an intervening variable
    (d) not a variable at all
20. A big difference between the mean and median is an indication that
    (a) There is a mistake in the calculation
    (b) the calculation is correct
    (c) there is a wide variation in the data
    (d) None of the above
21. Which of the following research methods is useful in a study on measuring the active life of periodicals
    (a) Survey **(b) Citation Analysis**
    (c) Interview (d) Case Study

22. Which of the following types of memory is volatile
    (a) ROM (b) PROM
    (c) WORM **(d) RAM**
23. Which of the following is not a programming language?
    (a) FORTRAN (b) BASIC
    (c) COBOL **(d) ASCII**
24. When you creat a worksheet in CDS/ISIS you are defining
    (a) the external user view
    (b) the internal file structure
    (c) the conceptual frame
    (d) all of the above
25. UNESCO's information programme is known as
    (a) NATIS **(b) PGI**
    (c) UAP (d) UBC
26. Which of the following networks does not have its own telecommunication infrastructure
    (a) NICNET (b) ERNET
    (c) INIS (d) EURONET
27. OPAC stands for
    (a) Online Public Access Catalogue
    (b) Online Periodicals Access Centre
    (c) Online Patents Access
    (d) None of the above
28. In a communication model noise refers to
    (a) Loudness of signal
    (b) lack of understanding between sender and receiver
    (c) any disturbances which affect the transmission
    (d) irrelevant information
29. Zero growth libraries contradict fifth law of library science. The statement is
    (a) True, because no new books are added
    (b) true, because the total size of the book stock is steady
    (c) false, since the library may grow in other ways

(d) false, since there can be no zero growth libraries

30. SENDOC is the national centre for
    (a) Science and Environment
    (b) Sociology and Economics
    (c) Sri Lanka
    (d) Small Scale Enterprise
31. Extension services to the blind by public library is justified by
    (a) the fourth law of library science
    (b) the first law of library science
    (c) the fifth law of library science
    (d) **all the laws of library science**
32. The table standard subdivision helps a classification scheme
    (a) To ensure consistency
    (b) **To add mnemonic value**
    (c) Both the above
    (d) None of the above
33. Which of the following names are associated with post co-ordinate indexing
    (a) **Taube, Mooers, Batten**
    (b) Taube, Austin, Coates
    (c) Taube, Austin, Garfield
    (d) Mooers, Taube, Garfield
34. A document description is not found in a
    (a) Catalogue entry (b) Citation
    (c) Bibliographic Entry (d) **Class number**
35. The following is not an example of repackaging of information
    (a) Trend report (b) **Catalogue**
    (c) Summary (d) Digest
36. In UDC, the inter-relationship between two subjects denoted by
    (a) Ampersand followed by Roman smalls
    (b) **A colon**
    (c) Double colon (d) Hyphen

37. GOC helps libraries in determining
    (a) **Foreign exchange rates**
    (b) Names of foreign agents and vendors
    (c) Books available in the market
    (d) Which books to buy
38. In a library which of the following positions are line positions
    (i) Junior library assistant
    (ii) Subject specialist
    (iii) Deputy Librarian
    (iv) Systems librarians
    (a) (i) and (ii) **(b) (i) and (iii)**
    (c) (i) and (iv) (d) (ii) and (iv)
39. An organisational structure is determined by
    (i) Span of control (ii) Hierarchy
    (iii) Space and location
    (a) **(i) and (ii)** (b) (ii) and (iii)
    (c) (i) and (iii) (d) All the factors
40. According to AACR-II, the heading of the main entry for conference proceeding edited by an individual is prepared under
    (a) Name of editor (b) Place of conference
    (c) Title of the volume (d) Name of the conference
41. Indian National Bibliography does not include
    (a) Books published in India in English
    (b) **Official reports**
    (c) Books on India, published abroad
    (d) Books published in recognised Indian languages
42. The subject headings 'money' and 'inflation' are both used in a retrieval system
    (a) **Be linked by a 'see also' reference**
    (b) Be linked by 'see' reference
    (c) Be linked by both 'see' and 'see also' reference
    (d) Not be linked
43. The resource sharing strategy of a library may not include

(a) Joint acquisition (b) Shared use
(c) Exchange of materials (d) Restricted access

44. Which of the following is not a national library?
(a) Library of Congress (b) British Library
(c) Bibliotheque Nationale (d) **Smithsonian Institute**

45. UNESCO Public Library manifesto was last revised in
(a) 1990 (b) 1998
(c) 1997 **(d) 1994 <latest 2001>**

46. The ICCP did not lead to
(a) Agreement on the need for uniformity and standards
(b) a definition of main entry
(c) a recognition of corporate authorship
(d) the development of MARC format

47. In KWIC index the keyword appears
(a) At the beginning of each entry
(b) at the centre of the line
(c) as the highlighted word
(d) at the end of the line

48. The relationship between the terms 'Ships' and "Boat" is
(a) Syntactic relation (b) semantic relation
(c) Both of them (d) Neither

49. Which of the following cannot be regarded as multimedia
(a) A tape-slide program
(b) A CD-ROM with text and visual
(c) Microfilm
(d) A Web page

50. Invisible colleges
(a) Networks of people interested in the same subject
(b) Help in communication
(c) neither (A) nor (b)
(d) **both (a) and (b)**

December 2000

1. The headquarters of Raja Rammohan Roy Library Foundation is situated at
   (a) Delhi **(b) Calcutta**
   (c) Chennai (d) Nagpur
2. The first library act was passed and implemented in
   (a) Maharashtra (b) Andhra
   (c) Madras (d) Karnataka
3. A number of devices that are related to recal and precision have been studied by
   (a) Gilchrist (b) Vickery
   (c) Lancaster (d) Ranganathan
4. User studies in Social Sciences were carried out by
   (a) Kuhn **(b) Brittain**
   (c) Line (d) Allen
5. An entry that is made for the subject of a chapter in a book is referred to as
   (a) Cross Reference Entry
   (b) Cross Reference Index Entry
   (c) Class Index Entry
   (d) Book Index Entry
6. The concept of UBC was introduced by
   (a) UNESCO (b) LC
   (c) FID **(d) IFLA**
7. In Sears List of Subject Headings preferred headings are indicated by
   (a) Making them as preferred heading
   (b) Printing them in bold type
   (c) Underlining them
   (d) Italicising them
8. The component of an ISO-2709 meant primarily machine processing of the record is
   (a) the Label **(b) the Directory**
   (c) the Datafields (d) the record Separator
9. The CCF was developed by

(a) LC **(b) UNESCO**
(c) IFLA (d) FID

10. The agency in India is responsible for assigning ISSN
    (a) The National Library
    (b) INSDOC
    (c) INFLIBNET
    (d) Raja Rammohan Roy Educational Resource Centre

11. The concept of scientific management was introduced by
    (a) Henry fayol (b) C.I.Bernard
    (c) Peter Drucker **(d) F.W.Taylor**

12. Preparation, service, assimilation are the main stages involved in
    (a) Initiation (b) User Education
    (c) Reference Service **(d) Bibliography**

13. Desirableness of personal contact between reader and library material is stressed by
    (a) H.P.Luhn (b) Derek Austin
    (c) Samuel H.Green (d) S.C.Bradford

14. 'Informatics' is a term which was first use for documentation in
    (a) Britain **(b) USA (M.F.Collen, 1994)**
    (c) USSR/Russia (d) India

15. Intellectual Property Rights are recognised by
    (a) Copyright (b) Patent
    (c) Both (d) neither

16. Identify the primary document from the following
    (a) Bibliography (b) Biography
    (c) Autobiography **(d) None of the above**

17. Identify the secondary source from the following
    (a) Standards (b) Patents (b) Journals
    (d) Directories

18. The procedures for chain indexing was developed by
    (a) Jack Mills (b) C.A.Cutter
    (c) S.R.Ranganathan (d) G.Bhattacharya

19. NATIS stands for
    (a) National Information System
    (b) National Technical Information System
    (c) National Team for Information Science
    (d) None of the above
20. MESH is the name of a
    (a) Medical Library
    (b) CSIR Unit
    (c) Controlled Vocabulary
    (d) None of the above
21. POPSI was developed by
    (a) S.R.Ranganathan (b) A.Neelameghan
    (c) B.S.Kesavan **(d) G.Bhattacharya**
22. According to CCC, the heading for work with three authors is
    (a) The first author (b) The title
    (c) The principal author (d) All the three authors
23. Which of the following area is not a part of the description prescribed by AACR-II?
    (a) Title and statement of responsibility area
    (b) Edition
    (c) Publication and distribution
    (d) address and location
24. Paul Otlet used the term 'Documentation' for the first time in a lecture at the International Congress at Brussels in
    (a) 1905 (b) 1920
    (c) 1931 (d) 1948
25. ISBN contains
    (a) 6 digits
    (b) 8 digits
    (c) 10 digits
    (d) 12 digits **<presently 13 digits>**
26. BNB is published
    (a) Weekly (b) Monthly
    (c) Bi-monthly (d) Annual

27. Principles of later-in-time is one of the
    (a) Five Laws of Library Science
    (b) Cataloguing Principles
    (c) Principles of Helpful Sequence
    (d) Circulation Rules
28. European Translation Centre is located at
    (a) Italy (b) France
    (c) Netherland (d) Germany
29. Micropaedia is in how many volumes?
    (a) 5 **(b) 10**
    (c) 12 (d) 20
30. 'Facts on File' is published from
    (a) India
    (b) Africa
    (c) USA <leading publishers from 1941>
    (d) Europe
31. Which table deals with 'standard Subdivisions' in DDC?
    (a) Table 1 (b) Table 3
    (c) Table 5 (d) Table 7
32. What is Bibliography
    (a) A list of Books published
    (b) A list of books available in a library
    (c) A list of books available in two library
    (d) A list of journals
33. Bibliographic service comes under
    (a) Ready Reference Service
    (b) Long Range Service
    (c) Referral Service
    (d) None of the above
34. McGraw-Hill is a
    (a) Author (b) Printer
    (c) Publisher (d) Librarian
35. 'Indian Science Abstract' is published by
    (a) INSDOC (presently NISCAIR)
    (b) ICSSR

(c) DST
(d) DRTC

36. Library week is celebrated on
(a) 10th November **(b) 14th November**
(c) 14th December (d) 25th December

37. Encyclopaedia Britannica is in how many parts
(a) Single (b) Two
(c) Three (d) Four

38. State the number of tables DDC includes
(a) 3 (b) 5
(c) 7 (d) 9

39. Saraswati Mahal Library at
(a) Tanjore (b) Bhubaneswar
(c) Jaipur (d) Thiruvananthapuram

40. Association is a
(a) Personal Author (b) Pseudonymous Author
(c) Periodical Publication **(d) Corporate author**

41. As per CC 'm' refers to
(a) Anteriorising Common Isolate
(b) Posteriorising Common Isolate
(c) Time isolate
(d) Useful Arts

42. Library of Congress is located at
(a) Washington, DC (b) Chicago
(c) New York (d) London

43. If in the year 2000, a journal has reached its 40th volume, when was it first published
(a) 1959 (b) 1960
(c) 1961 (d) None of the above

44. Connemara Public Library was established after the name of the then
(a) Governor (b) Judge
(c) King (d) Philanthropist

45. The real name of 'Mark Twain' is
(a) Milton (b) Keats

(c) Samuel Langhorne Clemens
(d) William Wordsworth

46. Windows NT is the name of
(a) Cable TV
(b) Network
(c) A Computer Operating System
(d) an online database

47. Lexicon refers to
(a) Bibliography **(b) Dictionary**
(c) Encyclopedia (d) Directory

48. To find an occurance of a term in a work which part of the work you refer
(a) Contents (b) Chapters
(c) Index (d) Title

49. The term 'thesaurus' is associated with
(a) Directory (b) Bibliography
(c) Dictionary (d) None of the above

50. CLRI (Central Leather Research Institute) is located at
(a) Chennai (b) Calicut
(c) Cochin (d) Cuttack

NET Paper II : SOLUTIONS

(2005-2010) (New Pattern)

(All Answers in Bold Letters)

YEAR WISE ARRANGEMENT

June 2005

1. The fundamental equation of Information Science has been put forward by:
   (a) Michael Buckland **(b) Robert Brooks**
   (c) Marc Porat (d) Wersig Gernot
2. Source, Message, Transmitter and Receiver are the components of communication model
   (a) Shannon-Weaver (b) Schramm
   (c) Lasswell (d) George Gerbner
3. Who said that Knowledge is of two kinds. We know a subject ourselves or we know where we can find information about it?
   (a) S.R.Ranganathan (b) W.C.Berwick Sayers
   (c) Samuel Johnson (d) H.E.Bliss
4. The acronym for Association for Information management is:
   (a) IAMA (b) AIM
   (c) ASLIB (d) IIM
5. Census Atlas National Volume is an example of __________ Atlas:
   (a) Local (b) Historical
   (c) Demographic (d) Anthropologocal
6. COMPENDEX is the on-line Database on the subject:
   (a) Physics (b) Commerce and Export
   (c) Analytical Chemistry **(d) Engineering**
7. Routing of periodicals is:
   (a) CAS (b) SDI
   (c) Indexing Service (d) Abstracting Service
8. The subject 'Research Methodology' has been formed by which of the following modes?
   (a) Fusion **(b) Distillation**
   (c) Fission (d) Loose Assemblage
9. Boolean Logic was propounded by:
   (a) B.C.Vickery (b) S.C.Bradford
   (c) J.Buckland **(d) George Boole**

10. 'IMCE' stands for:
    (a) International Meeting of Cataloguing Experts
    (b) International Meeting of Computer Experts
    (c) International Meeting of Communication Experts
    (d) International Meeting of Classification Experts
11. An indispensable function of Thesaurus is:
    (a) Knowledge representation
    (b) Problem solving
    (c) Representation of relationship between concepts
    (d) Knowledge engineering
12. 'Book Number' helps in:
    (a) Individualising the book within the same class number
    (b) Individualising the book among the books with same authors
    (c) Individualising among the books with same year of publication
    (d) Knowing the subject of the book
13. The library budget prepared without considering the previous years budget is:
    (a) Zerobased Budget (b) Performance Budget
    (c) Line item Budget (d) Lumpsum Budget
14. The abbreviation MB to state the storage capacity refers to:
    (a) Mega bytes (b) Million Bits
    (c) Million bytes (d) mega bits
15. Data about data is known as:
    (a) Micro data (b) Database
    (c) Metadata (d) Databank
16. The concept of Micro photography was developed by:
    (a) Johan Gutenberg
    (b) Chester cardson
    (c) John Benjamin Dancer (1839)
    (d) Ohi Battle
17. Which among the following is a digital library software used in the creation of an inhouse digital library

(a) LIBSYS **(b) Greenstone**
(c) Alice for Windows (d) Micro CDS/ISIS

18. SSDC referred to the National Documentation Centre now known as:
(a) DESIDOC (b) SENDOC
(c) NISCOM **(d) NASSDOC**

19. Annual Convention of INFLIBNET organised to discuss the progress of the library automation and library services is known as:
(a) ISCON (b) NACLIN
(c) CALIBER (d) INFONET

20. Formulation of Research Hypothesis implies:
(a) Creating a legal basis for research
(b) Enunciation of Postulates
(c) Enumeration of canons
(d) Formation of tentative generalization

21. The study of Epistomology deals with:
(I) Modes of formation of subjects
(II) Classification of knowledge
(III) Cataloguing of composite books
(IV) Origin, source and nature of knowledge
In the type of items, there may be more than one answer. Identify the correct combination:
(a) I and II are correct
(b) II and III are correct
(c) I, II and III are correct
(d) II and IV are correct

22. The Compact Disk is conceptually referred to as:
(I) Magnetic storage (II) Compact storage
(III) Optical storage (IV) All the above
In the type of items, there may be more than one answer. Identify the correct combination:
(a) I, II and III are correct
(b) II and III are correct
(c) I and III are correct
(d) (II) and (IV) are correct

23. Match the following:

	List-I (Abbreviation)	**List-II (Meaning)**
I.	Ibid	a. See
II.	Loc. Cit.	b. Previously cited
III.	Op.cit.	c. Same reference cited immediately above
IV.	Vide	d. The same place cited

Codes:

(a) I-a, II-b, III-C, IV-d (b) I-b, II-a, III-d, IV-c

(c) I-c, II-d, III-b, IV-a (d) I-d, II-c, III-a, IV-b

24. Match the following:

	List-I *(Types of users of information)*	**List-II** *(Purpose of use of information)*
I.	Students	a. Decision making
II.	Professionals	b. To impart knowledge
III.	Government Officials	c. To prepare for the course programme
IV.	Teachers	d. To pursue their respective vocation

Codes:

(a) I-c, II-d, III-a, IV-b

(b) I-d, II-a, III-b, IV-c

(c) I-c, II-b, III-d, IV-a

(d) I-b, II-b, III-c, IV-d

25. Match the following:

	List-I (Writing materials)	**List-II (Place of origin)**
I.	Clay Tablet	a. Algeria/Babylonia
II.	Palm Leaves	b. Egypt
III.	Paper	c. Ninveh
IV.	Papyrus	d. China
		e. India

Codes:

(a) I-c, II-b, III-a, IV-d **(b) I-d, II-e, III-a, IV-c**
(c) I-c, II-e, III-d, IV-b (d) I-c, II-b, III-a, IV-d

26. Match the following:

	List-I (Database)	**List-II (Supplier)**
I.	ERIC	a. American Chemical Society, USA
II.	C.A.Search	b. Bowker & Saur London
III.	Books in Print	c. R.R.Bowker USA
IV.	LISA	d. National Institute of Education, USA

Codes:

(a) I-d, II-a, III-c, IV-b (b) I-d, II-b, III-a, IV-c
(c) I-b, II-c, III-a, IV-d (d) I-a, II-d, III-b, IV-b

27. Match the following:

	List-I	**List-II**
I.	ILRC (Inter Library Resource Centre)	a. Science and Technology
II.	NISSAT	b. Indexing Service
III.	Journal of Librarianship	c. UK
IV.	INIS Atomindex	d. Delhi

Codes:

(a) I-a, II-b, III-d, IV-c (b) I-b, II-c, III-a, IV-d
(c) I-d, II-a, III-c, IV-b (d) I-c, II-d, III-d, IV-a

28. Match the following:

	List-I	**List-II**
I.	POPSI	a. P.M.Roget
II.	Citation Indexing	b. H.P.Luhn
III.	Keyword Indexing	c. Eugene Garfield
IV.	Thesaurus	d. G.Bhattacharyya

Codes:

(a) I-b, II-d, III-a, IV-c (b) I-c, II-d, III-a, IV-b
(c) I-d, II-c, III-b, IV-a (d) I-a, II-b, III-d, IV-c

29. Match the following:

	List-I	List-II
I.	DDC	a. J.D.Brown
II.	Expansive Classification	b. H.E.Bliss
III.	Subject Classification	c. Melvil Dewey
IV.	Bibliographic classification	d. C.A.Cutter

Codes:

(a) I-b, II-d, III-c, IV-a (b) I-c, II-b, III-a, IV-d
(c) I-a, II-b, III-d, IV-c **(d) I-c, II-d, III-a, IV-b**

30. Match the following:

	List-I (Technical Terms)	List-II (Meaning)
I.	Thesaurus	a. Collection of programmes for the Computer System
II.	Windows	b. A revolving disc on which data is stored
III.	Microprocessors	c. A graphical user interface created as DOS Extension by Microsoft
IV.	Software	d. A multi user Operating System
		e. A classified dictionary of synonyms

Codes:

(a) I-b, II-d, III-c, IV-a (b) I-c, II-e, III-a, IV-d
(c) I-e, II-c, III-b, IV-a (d) I-c, II-d, III-a, IV-b

31. Match the following:

	List-I	List-II
I.	Browser	a. Google
II.	Operating System	b. 'C'
III.	Programming language	c. Internet Explorer
IV.	Search Engine	d. Windows

Codes:

(a) I-a, II-c, III-b, IV-d (b) I-c, II-b, III-d, IV-a
(c) I-c, II-d, III-b, IV-a (d) I-d, II-b, III-c, IV-a

32. Match the following:

	List-I	**List-II**
I.	INIS	a. Ohio
II.	AGRIS	b. Delhi
III.	OCLC	c. Vienna
IV.	NICNET	d. Rome

Codes:

(a) I-c, II-a, III-b, IV-d (b) I-b, II-d, III-c, IV-a
(c) I-d, II-c, III-a, IV-b **(d) I-c, II-d, III-a, IV-b**

33. Match the following:

	List-I	**List-II**
I.	Observation	a. Knowledge
II.	Organization (Logical Relation)	b. Data/Ideas
III.	Learning and Assimilation	c. Wisdom
IV.	Judgement (application of content)	d. Information

Codes:

(a) I-d, II-a, III-c, IV-b (b) I-c, II-b, III-d, IV-a
(c) I-a, II-c, III-b, IV-d **(d) I-b, II-d, III-a, IV-c**

34. Match the following:

	List-I	**List-II**
I.	Mysticism	a. Y7
II.	Useful Arts	b. Y
III.	Sociology	c. ?
IV.	Anthropology	d. M

Codes:

(a) I-c, II-d, III-b, IV-a (b) I-d, II-b, III-c, IV-a
(c) I-b, II-c, III-d, IV-a (d) I-a, II-d, III-c, IV-b

35. **Assertion (a):** Library cooperation is the prime need of the day.

Reason (R): It is impossible for an individual library to meet all the requirements of its users.

(a) Both A and R are true and R is the correct explanation

(b) Both A and R are true and R is not the correct explanation

(c) A is true but R is false

(d) A is false but R is true

36. Which one of the following pairs is NOT correctly matched?

(a) The difference between the highest and lowest values of a variable.....Range

(b) The value of a variable which divides the area under the frequency curve into two equal parts ......Median

(c) The result when the sum of all the terms in the series is divided by the number of items in the series.......Mean

(d) **The value of a variable for which the frequency is maximum ..... Probability**

37. **Asertion (a):** Arrangement of documents by subject will satisfy more users.

Reason (R): Many users search for documents by title.

(a) Both A and R are true and R is the correct explanation

(b) Both A and R are true and R is not the correct explanation

(c) A is true but R is false

(d) A is false but R is true

38. **Assertion (a):** A special library serves a specialist clientele.

Reason (R): The collection of special library is relatively narrow in scope

(a) Both A and R are true and R is the correct explanation

(b) A and R are true and R is not the correct explanation

(c) A is true but R is false

(d) A is false but R is true

39. **Assertion (a):** Copyright Act safeguards the interest of the author.

Reason (R): The Act is essential to maximise the circulation of documents

(a) Both A and R are true and R is the correct explanation

(b) A and R are true and R is not the correct explanation

(c) A is true but R is false

(d) A is false but R is true

40. Arrange the following classification schemes according to the year of publication use the code below:

I. Colon Classification (1933)

II. Dewey Decimal Classification (1876)

III. Bibliographic Classification (1935)

IV. Sibject Classification (1905)

Codes:

(a) II, IV, I, III (b) III, II, I, IV

(c) I, IV, III, II (d) IV, II, III, I

41. Identify the correct chronological order in which they were setup:

(a) NASSDOC, RRRLF, DRTC, INSDOC

(b) RRRLF, INSDOC, NASSDOC, DRTC

(c) **INSDOC(1952), DRTC (1962), NASSDOC (1970), RRRLF (1972)**

(d) DRTC, INSDOC, NASSDOC, RRRLF

42. Arrange the following units of storage capacity in increasing order of magnitude. Use the code given below:

I. Gigabyte II. Kilobyte

III. Terabyte IV. Megabyte

Codes:

(a) IV, II, III, I (b) I, III, II, IV

(c) III, IV, I, II **(d) II, IV, I, III**

43. Based on the years of establishment arrange the following in chronological order. Use the code given below:

I. ASLIB (1924) II. ALA (1876)

III. ILA (1933) IV. IFLA (1927)

Codes:

(a) III, IV, II, I (b) I, IV, III, II

(c) II, I, IV, III (d) IV, I, III, II

44. Identify the correct order in which the commission were set up. Use the code given below:

I. Roy Committee on StateUniversities Review

II. Radhakrishnan Commission on Education (1948)

III. Kothari Commission on Education (1964)

IV. Mudaliar Commission of Secondary Education (1953)

Codes:

(a) I, IV, III, II (b) IV, III, I, II

(c) III, II, I, IV **(d) II, IV, III, I**

45. Arrange the following components in order in which they were used in computers. Use the code given below:

I. Transistors (2nd gen.)

II. Vacuum Tubes (1st gen.)

III. Large Scale Integrated Circuit (3rd gen.)

IV. Very Large Scale Integrated Circuit (4th gen.)

Codes:

(a) I, III, II, IV **(b) II, I, III, IV**

(c) II, III, IV, I (d) IV, I, III, II

COMPREHENSION TEST

46. (a) **The growth of the Internet and its ubiquitous use in study and work creates new areas of concern. The most important one being information literacy in higher education.**

(b) The growth of the Internet enables people pursuing higher education. Information literate helps them in their study and work.

(c) Internet use in higher education promotes

information literacy and provides complete information resource.

(d) Students who use the Internet gain real confidence in the Internet as a complete information source.

47. (a) Information once recorded into the web remains static and can be utilized by the users of the web as and when they need it.

(b) **The Web may have "changed everything", but in doing so it has created a new problem of information illiteracy; that of false confidence in the internet as a complete information resource.**

(c) The students of higher education may rely completely on Internet resources.

(d) Students who completely rely on the Internet uniformly do not lack understanding about the resources available to them.

48. (a) The large volume of content available on Internet across a range of areas does not create any " Information anxiety" in the users of the Internet.

(b) Information available on the Web across subject areas is of manageable proportions and does not bewilder the users of the Internet.

(c) **There is proliferation of content across such range of areas, available with such immediacy that the sheer volume of information can seem overwhelming ... and may cause "Information anxiety".**

(d) It is easy to find relevant and useful information across a range of areas from the web without getting oneself bewildered.

49. (a) **The most significant challenge to the information profession in information society is to map and signpost the information landscape. This has been the traditional role of the librarian and whilest the information domain is changing the core principles of the**

profession remain as important to society.

(b) The Internet does not pose significant challenges to the information profession.

(c) The role of librarians is not to map and signpost the information landscape.

(d) While the information domain is changing the core principles of the profession also should change.

50. (a) Retrieving pertinent information from the Internet is not demanding of the information seeker in the formulation of search terms and almost always produces vast number of hits.

(b) There is no user friendly search engine to help the information seeker to access pertinent information necessary for his work.

(c) The quality of information retrieved from the Internet is of high precision and does not pose problems to the user.

(d) 'Information anxiety' created by the bewildering nature of Internet is made simple by the user friendly quality associated with Google search interface. This interface acts as a tonic and helps the information seeker even with spelling.

June 2006

1. Which among the following is considered as an informal channel of Information Communication?

(a) Journals (b) Textbooks

(c) Invisible Colleges (d) Technical Reports

2. Which one of the following is not correctly matched?

(a) Books in Print – Trade Bibliography

(b) Cummulative Book Index – Books published in English language

(c) British Books in Print – R.R.Bowker

(d) National Bibliography – INB

3. URL stands for:

(a) Uniform Resource Locator

(b) Universal Resource Locator
(c) Unified Resource Locator
(d) Uniform Reference Locator

4. Zero Based Budgeting system was propounded by:
(a) Peter Drucker (b) Edward Evans
(c) Allent Kent **(d) Peter Phyrr**

5. A series of interconnected documents stored on the Internet is called:
(a) Websites (b) Domain Name
(c) Home Page (d) Web Page

6. The first All India Conference of Librarians in 1918 was held at:
(a) Baroda (b) Calcutta
(c) Madras (d) Lahore

7. If two citations are called together, it is known as:
(a) Double citation (b) Twin citation
(c) Co-citation (d) Controlled citation

8. Grey literature means:
(a) The literature published by a publisher named as "Grey Publisher"
(b) The literature which is not published and is not available through normal book selling channels
(c) The literature published and made available in Grey shades
(d) The literature which is published and made available through special publishers

9. The smallest unit of data in a database is:
(a) Record (b) File
(c) Field (d) Table

10. The term 'Bandwidth' refers to:
(a) The amount of data that can be sent through communication media
(b) The amount of data in a multimedia file
(c) The speed of transmission of data
(d) Number of bands available in a computer

11. Which of the following factors is not considered in the making of a library budget?
    (a) The size of the organiation
    (b) The type of users
    (c) The collection
    (d) The age of library employees
12. OCLC is:
    (i) Online Computer Library Center
    (ii) At Dublin (Ohio)
    (iii) At New York
    (iv) Ohio College Library Center
    (a) (i) and (ii) are correct
    (b) (i) and (iii) are correct
    (c) (iii) and (iv) are correct
    (d) (ii) and (iv) are correct
13. Pre-coordinate indexing system is followed in:
    (i) Chain Indexing (ii) POPSI
    (iii) UNITERM (iv) PRECIS
    (a) (i) and (iv) are correct
    (b) (i) (ii) and (iii) are correct
    (c) (i) (ii) and (iv) are correct
    (d) (ii) and (iv) are correct
14. ADONIS is a:
    (i) Bibliographic database only
    (ii) Numerical database only
    (iii) Full text database
    (iv) None of the above
    (a) (i) and (ii) are correct (b) (ii) and (iii) are correct
    (c) (iii) is correct (d) (iv) is correct
15. Hypothesis is a:
    (i) Solution to the problems
    (ii) Statement of assumption
    (iii) Statement to be tested
    (iv) Fact
    (a) (i) and (iii) are correct **(b) (ii) and (iii) are correct**

(c) (i) and (ii) are correct (d) (i) and (iv) are correct

16. The first library science school in the world was started
    (i) By Melvil Dewey
    (ii) At Columbia University, New York (USA)
    (iii) By W.C.Berwick Sayers
    (iv) At London University, London (UK)
    (a) (i) and (ii) are correct
    (b) (i) and (iv) are correct
    (c) (ii) and (iii) are correct
    (d) (iii) and (iv) are correct
17. Primary sources include:
    (i) Thesis (ii) Patent
    (iii) Abstracting Periodical (iv) Periodical Article
    (a) (i) (ii) and (iii) are correct
    (b) (i) (iii) and (iv) are correct
    (c) (i) (ii) and (iv) are correct
    (d) (ii) (ii) and (iv) are correct
18. Shannon and Weaver are associated with:
    (i) Mathematical theory of communication
    (ii) Models of communication
    (iii) Theories of Management
    (iv) Library software packages
    (a) (i) and (ii) are correct
    (b) (i) and (iii) are correct
    (c) (ii) and (iii) are correct
    (d) (ii) and (iv) are correct
19. The decision to make or not to make an entry under a subject term is governed by the
    (a) Canon of Ascertainability
    (b) Canon of Prepotence
    (c) Canon of Sought Heading
    (d) Canon of Context
20. Span of control refers to:
    (a) The numbers of subordinates to be supervised
    (b) Exercise strict control staff

(c) Duration over which the control is to be exercised
(d) The area which is to be controlled

21. **Assertion (a):** Classification as a tool for organisation of knowledge will continue to persist

Reason (R): In the age of e-documents classification is redundant.

Codes:

(a) Both (a) and (R) are true
(b) (a) is correct and (R) is false
(c) (R) is correct and (a) is false
(d) Both (a) and (R) are false

22. **Assertion (a):** Collection development should be judiciously done.

Reason (R): Almost all libraries have limited resources

Codes:

(a) Both (a) and (R) are true and (R) is the correct explanation
(b) Both (a) and (R) are true but (R) is not the right explanation
(c) (a) is true but (R) is false
(d) (a) is false but (R) is true

23. **Assertion (a):** No single library connect all the demands of the users

Reason (R): Resource sharing is the need of the day.

Codes:

(a) Both (a) and (R) are false
(b) Both (a) and (R) are correct
(c) (a) is false but (R) is true
(d) (R) is false but (a) is true

24. **Assertion (a):** Library catalogues meet most of the approaches of the users.

Reason (R): Catalogues include all the details of the document

Codes:

(a) Both (a) and (R) are true
(b) (a) is true but (R) are false
(c) Both are partially true
(d) (R) is true and (a) is false

25. **Assertion (a)**: Information can be obtained from several sources other than the libraries.
Reason (R): Library science is narrower in scope than information science

Codes:

(a) (a) is false and (R) are true
(b) (R) is false and (a) is true
(c) Both (a) and (R) are false
(d) Both (a) and (R) are true

26. The catalogue codes were developed in the order as:
(a) Anglo American Code (Joint Code), Rules for Dictionary Catalogue, ALA rules for author and title entries, AACRI
(b) Rules for Dictionary Catalogue, ALA rules for author and title entries, AACRI, Anglo American Code (Joint Code),
(c) **Rules for Dictionary Catalogue (1876), Anglo American Code (Joint Code) (1904), ALA rules for author and title entries (1942), AACRI (1967)**
(d) ALA rules for author and title entries, AACRI, Rules for Dictionary Catalogue, Anglo American Code (Joint Code)

27. Which is the correct sequence of the following in the chronological order of publication
(a) 14th edition of DDC, 1st edition of CC, Rider's International Classification, Broad System of Ordering
(b) 1st edition of CC, 14th edition of DDC, Broad System of Ordering, Rider's International Classification
(c) Rider's International Classification, 1st edition of

CC, 14th edition of DDC, Broad System of Ordering

(d) 1st edition of CC(1934), **Rider's International Classification, 14th edition of DDC** (1942), **Broad System of Ordering** (1978)

28. Identify the development in following library software in correct chronological sequence
    (a) Sanjaya, LibSys SLIM, SOUL
    (b) SLIM, LibSys, SOUL, Sanjaya
    (c) Libsys, Sanjaya, SOUL, SLIM
    (d) Sanjaya, SOUL, SLIM, LibSys
29. Select the right chronological sequence of information systems as per their year of establishment
    (a) INIS, AGRIS, NISSAT, Patent Information System (India)
    (b) AGRIS, NISSAT, INIS, Patent Information System (India)
    (c) **Patent Information System (India), INIS, AGRIS, NISSAT**
    (d) NISSAT, AGRIS, INIS, Patent Information System (India)
30. Select the right sequences of the following devices according to their storage capacity in descending order:
    (a) CD, DVD, Floppy Disc, Punched Card
    (b) Floppy Disc, Punched card, CD, DVD
    (c) Punched Card, Floppy Disc, CD, DVD
    (d) DVD, CD, Floppy Disc, Punched Card
31. Select the right sequence of contribution of classificationists in the chronological order
    (a) **Francis Bacon (17th century), W.T.Harris (1870), Melvil Dewey (1876), J.D.Brown (1905)**
    (b) W.T.Harris, Francis Bacon, Melvil Dewey, J.D.Brown
    (c) Francis Bacon, Melvil Dewey, J.D.Brown, W.T.Harris
    (d) Francis Bacon, J.D.Brown, W.T.Harris, Melvil Dewey

32. Arrange the contributors in management in the proper chronological order:

(i) Peter Drucker (ii) Henry Gantt

(iii) Ishikawa (iv) Juran

Codes:

	(i)	(ii)	(iii)	(iv)
(a)	Peter Drucker,	Henry Gantt,	Juran,	Ishikawa
(b)	Henry Gantt,	Peter Drucker	Juran,	Ishikawa
(c)	Henry Gantt,	Juran,	Ishikawa,	Peter Drucker
(d)	Ishikawa,	Henry Gantt,	Juran,	Peter Drucker

33. Arrange the following in the chronological sequence:

(i) CCF (ii) Metadata

(iii) ISBD (iv) MARC

Codes:

(a) **(iv) (iii) (i) (ii)** (b) (iii) (iv) (i) (ii)

(c) (i) (iii) (iv) (ii) (d) (iii) (i) (iv) (ii)

34. Match the following:

	List-I	**List-II**
(a)	Zipf's Law	(i) Impact factor
(b)	Lotka's Law	(ii) Circulation Statistics
(c)	Bradford's Law	(iii) Author Productivity
(d)	Eugene Garfield	(iv) Word frequency
		(v) Scattering

Codes:

	(a)	(b)	(c)	(d)
(a)	(ii)	(iv)	(v)	(i)
(b)	(v)	(i)	(iv)	(ii)
(c)	**(iv)**	**(iii)**	**(v)**	**(i)**
(d)	(iii)	(iv)	(v)	(ii)

35. Match the following:

	List-I	**List-II**
(a)	SOUL	(i) DESIDOC

	List-I	List-II
(b)	WINISIS	(ii) ALGORITHM
(c)	SANJAY	(iii) Informatics (India)
(d)	SLIM	(iv) INFLIBNET
		(v) UNESCO

Codes:

	(a)	(b)	(c)	(d)
(a)	**(iv)**	**(v)**	**(i)**	**(ii)**
(b)	(v)	(iii)	(iv)	(i)
(c)	(iv)	(v)	(ii)	(iii)
(d)	(v)	(iv)	(i)	(ii)

36. Match the following:

	List-I	List-II
(a)	Kothari Commission	(i) Status and Pay scales of libraries
(b)	Radhakrishnan Commission	(ii) Public Library System
(c)	Mehrotra Commission	(iii) Library Budget as a percentage
(d)	Fyzee Commission	(iv) Importance of library in Academic Institutions
		(v) Special libraries

Codes:

	(a)	(b)	(c)	(d)
(a)	(iii)	(i)	(v)	(ii)
(b)	**(iii)**	**(iv)**	**(i)**	**(ii)**
(c)	(ii)	(iii)	(i)	(v)
(d)	(iv)	(iii)	(ii)	(i)

37. Match the following:

	List-I	List-II
(a)	Translation Service	(i) BLDSC
(b)	Information Repackaging Services	(ii) DELNET
(c)	Document Delivery Service	(iii) ITC

(d)	Library Networking	(iv) Information Analysis Centre (IAC)
		(v) DRTC

Codes:

	(a)	(b)	(c)	(d)
(a)	(ii)	(iv)	(i)	(iii)
(b)	**(iii)**	**(iv)**	**(i)**	**(ii)**
(c)	(v)	(iv)	(ii)	(i)
(d)	(iii)	(v)	(iv)	(ii)

38. Match the following

	List-I	List-II
(a)	Z39.50	(i) Standard for Document Description
(b)	ISO 9000	(ii) Standard for Library Building
(c)	ISO 2709	(iii) Information Retrieval
(d)	ISBD (G)	(iv) Quality Related Standards
		(v) Bibliographic Record Structure

Codes:

	(a)	(b)	(c)	(d)
(a)	**(iii)**	**(iv)**	**(v)**	**(i)**
(b)	(iv)	(v)	(ii)	(iii)
(c)	(v)	(iv)	(ii)	(i)
(d)	(iv)	(iii)	(v)	(ii)

39. Match the following:

	List-I	List-II
(a)	Classarus	(i) Jean Aitchinson
(b)	Relative Index	(ii) J.L.Ferradane
(c)	Thesauro facet	(iii) S.R.Ranganathan
(d)	Relational Indexing	(iv) G.Bhattacharya
		(v) Melville Dewey

Codes:

	(a)	(b)	(c)	(d)
(a)	(iii)	(i)	(ii)	(v)
(b)	**(iv)**	**(v)**	**(i)**	**(ii)**
(c)	(ii)	(v)	(i)	(iii)
(d)	(iii)	(ii)	(i)	(v)

40. Match the following:

	List-I	**List-II**
(a)	CCF	(i) OCLC
(b)	UNIMARC	(ii) American Library Association
(c)	DUBLIN CORE	(iii) Library of Congress
(d)	USMARC	(iv) Unesco
		(v) IFLA

Codes:

	(a)	(b)	(c)	(d)
(a)	(v)	(iv)	(i)	(iii)
(b)	**(iv)**	**(v)**	**(i)**	**(ii)**
(c)	(iii)	(v)	(iv)	(ii)
(d)	(ii)	(iv)	(v)	(i)

41. Match the following:

	List-I	**List-II**
	(a) Management Service	(i) Fission
(b)	Biophysics	(ii) Distillation
(c)	Gandhiana	(iii) Agglomeration
(d)	Life Sciences	(iv) Clustering
		(v) Fusion

Codes:

	(a)	(b)	(c)	(d)
(a)	**(ii)**	**(v)**	**(iv)**	**(iii)**
(b)	(ii)	(iv)	(i)	(iii)
(c)	(iv)	(v)	(ii)	(i)
(d)	(iii)	(v)	(i)	(ii)

42. Match the following:

	List-I (Library Act)	**List-II (Year of Enactment)**
(a)	Madras Public Libraries Act	(i) 1965
(b)	West Bengal Public Libraries Act	(ii) 1960
(c)	Andhra Pradesh Public Libraries Act	(iii) 1948
(d)	Karnataka Public Libraries Act	(iv) 1979

Codes:

	(a)	(b)	(c)	(d)
(a)	**(iii)**	**(iv)**	**(ii)**	**(i)**
(b)	(i)	(ii)	(iii)	(iv)
(c)	(iii)	(ii)	(iv)	(i)
(d)	(ii)	(i)	(iv)	(iii)

43. Match the following:

List-I (Publication)	List-II (Institution/System)
(a) AGRINDEX	(i) INSPEC
(b) ATOMINDEX	(ii) National Library of Medicine
(c) Physical Abstracts	(iii) AGRIS
(d) INDEX MEDICUS	(iv) INIS

Codes:

	(a)	(b)	(c)	(d)
(a)	(iv)	(i)	(iii)	(ii)
(b)	(i)	(iii)	(iv)	(ii)
(c)	**(iii)**	**(iv)**	**(i)**	**(ii)**
(d)	(i)	(ii)	(iii)	(iv)

44. Match the following:

List-I (Contribution)	List-II (Organisation)
(a) Public Library Manifesto	(i) DRTC
(b) POPSI	(ii) Library of Congress
(c) UDC	(iii) UNESCO
(d) MARC	(iv) FID

Codes:

	(a)	(b)	(c)	(d)
(a)	(i)	(ii)	(iii)	(iv)
(b)	(ii)	(i)	(iii)	(iv)
(c)	**(iii)**	**(i)**	**(iv)**	**(ii)**
(d)	(iv)	(ii)	(iii)	(i)

45. Match the following:

	List-I (Medium/Coneectivity)	List-II (Type)
(a)	Fax	(i) Optical Storage
(b)	CD-ROM	(ii) Magnetic Storage
(c)	Floppy Disk	(iii) Switching System
(d)	Circuit	(iv) Image transmission

Codes:

	(a)	(b)	(c)	(d)
(a)	**(iv)**	**(i)**	**(ii)**	**(iii)**
(b)	(ii)	(iii)	(i)	(iv)
(c)	(i)	(ii)	(iii)	(iv)
(d)	(iii)	(ii)	(i)	(iv)

COMPREHENSION TEST:

46. "Stock verification is a common practice in the following agencies only". Choose the correct answer to justify it:
   (a) Libraries, government offices and hospitals
   (b) Libraries, government offices and residences
   (c) Libraries, government offices and business houses
   (d) Government offices, business houses and hotels

47. "Annual stock taking is usually done in order to assess profit and loss". Choose the correct answer to justify it:
   (a) The statement is false
   (b) The statement is true
   (c) The statement is partially true only
   (d) None of the above statements are correct

48. Choose the correct answer from the following:
   (a) Stock articles are consumables
   (b) Stock articles remain no longer in use
   (c) Stock articles are not permanent
   (d) Stock articles are of permanent value

49. Choose the correct answer from the following:
   (a) Casual leaves of employees are not consumable
   (b) Casual leaves are subject to cumulation

(c) Casual leaves are not subject to cumulation
(d) casual leaves are not lapsable

50. Choose the right answer from the following:
The type writer is a stock article because
(a) It is a consumable
(b) Little importance is attached to it
(c) It is not a stationary article
(d) It is to be used up soon

December 2006

1. Herzberg's two factor theory deals with:
(a) Staff recruitment (b) Leadership
(c) Decision making **(d) Motivation**

2. Raja Rammohan Roy Library Foundation:
(i) Promotes public libraries
(ii) Located at Mumbai
(iii) Promotes school libraries
(iv) Located at Kolkata
(a) (i) and (ii) are correct **(b) (i) and (iv) are correct**
(c) (i) and (iii) are correct (d) (iii) and (iv) are correct

3. The "Principle of Literary Warrant" was propounded by:
(a) S.R.Ranganathan **(b) W.Hulme**
(c) Melvil Dewey (d) Derek De Solla Price

4. Pre-natal Cataloguing means:
(a) Simplified Cataloguing
(b) Pre-Publication Cataloguing
(c) Selective Cataloguing
(d) Shared Cataloguing

5. The author who defined Reference Service as the "Process of establishing contact between a reader and his documents in a personal way" is:
(a) W.A.Katz (b) L.Shores
(c) M.Hutchins (d) S.R.Ranganathan

6. Identify the odd one:
   (a) LISA
   (b) Psychological Abstracts
   (c) Index Medicus
   (d) World of Learning
7. WIPO stands for:
   (a) World Information and Patents Organisation
   (b) World Intellectual Property Organisation
   (c) World International Property Organisation
   (d) World Information Protection Organisation
8. Which of the following is not correctly matched?
   (a) DELNET – Telecommunication Network
   (b) Digital Library – Print Material
   (c) Thesaurus – List of Descriptors
   (d) ISBN – Serial Number
9. An entry in an Abstracting Journal consists of:
   (a) Bibliographic citation
   (b) An abstract and bibliographic citation
   (c) Annotation
   (d) Bibliographic citation, an abstract and initials of the abstractor
10. Technological Gatekeeper is:
    (i) An informal channel
    (ii) A term coined by T.J.Allen
    (iii) A formal channel
    (iv) A term coined by Derek De Solla Price
    (a) (i) and (ii) are correct
    (b) (i) and (iii) are correct
    (c) (ii) and (iii) are correct
    (d) (iii) and (iv) are correct
11. The National Library for the visually handicapped is located at:
    (a) Allahabad
    (b) Indore
    (c) Dehradun
    (d) Nainital
12. In which of the following network topologies, all the computers are connected to a central computers are connected to a central computer:

(a) Ring **(b) Star**
(c) Bus (d) Peer to Peer

13. If the size of the study populationis very small, the following sampling method will give better results:
(a) Purposive (b) Stratified
(c) Random (d) Census

14. Formatting a document in computer means:
(a) Editing the content
(b) Changing the appearance
(c) Adding new content
(d) Changing the font size only

15. Which of the following search devices will lead to an increase in the Recall output?
(a) Boolean 'And' (b) Boolean 'Not'
(c) Proximity Operators **(d) Truncation**

16. Orientation of library users is a kind of:
(a) Reference Service
(b) Referral Service
(c) Current Awareness Service
(d) Selective Dissemination of Information Service

17. Informal communication among knowledgeable persons is known as:
(a) Invisible college
(b) Information gatekeeper
(c) Communication gatekeeper
(d) Knowledge management

18. Which of the following are produced by Institute of Scientific Information:
(i) Science Citation Index (ii) Current Contents
(iii) Index Medicus (iv) Atom Index
(a) (i), (ii) and (iii) **(b) (i) and (ii) only**
(c) (ii) and (III) only (d) (i) and (iv) only

19. The term 'Precision' to measure the performance of Information Retrieval Systems was suggested by:
(a) S.R.Ranganathan **(b) F.W.Lancaster**
(c) Cyril Cleverdon (d) H.P.Luhn

20. The GMD in a catalogue entry according to AACR-II revised edition is given:
    (a) After the title proper
    (b) Before the title
    (c) After the statement of responsibility
    (d) Before the statement of responsibility

21. **Assertion (a):** Computerization of Public Libraries in India is slow.
    Reason (R): Non-availability of resources
    Codes:
    (a) (a) is true but (R) is false
    (b) (R) is true but (a) is false
    (c) Both (a) and (R) are true
    (d) Both (a) and (R) are false

22. **Assertion (a):** Reference service is the hub of all library activities.
    Reason (R): It is provided in the shortest possible time.
    Codes:
    (a) (a) is true but (R) is false.
    (b) (R) is true but (a) is false.
    (c) Both (a) and (R) are true, but (R) is not the right explanation of (a).
    (d) Both (a) and (R) are true and (R) is the right explanation

23. **Assertion (a):** Systems analysis identifies the flow of work.
    Reason (R): Systems analysis is not necessary if the library is to be automated.
    Codes:
    (a) Both (a) and (R) are correct
    (b) Both (a) and (R) are false
    (c) (a) is true and (R) is false
    (d) (R) is true and (a) is false

24. **Assertion (a):** Users can have access to large to large number of E-journals through

consortia.

Reason (R): Users are not aware of using web resources.

Codes:

(a) (a) is false and (R) is true

(b) (a) is true and (R) is false

(c) **Both (a) and (R) are true but (R) is not the right explanation of (a)**

(d) Both (a) and (R) are false

25. **Assertion (a):** Historical, Descriptive and Experimental Methods are scientific methods.

Reason (R): A scientific method is one that adopts a logical and systematic procedure.

Codes:

(a) (a) is true but (R) is false.

(b) Both (a) and (R) are true

(c) (a) is false but (R) is true

(d) Both (a) and (R) are true but (R) is not the correct explanation

26. The chronological sequence of the technology is:

(a) Telephone, Television, Satellite Communication, INTERNET

(b) Telephone, Satellite Communication, Television, INTERNET

(c) Telephone, Television, INTERNET, Satellite Communication

(d) Telephone, INTERNET, Television, Satellite Communication

27. Identify the correct order of the evolution of the following storage devices:

(a) DVD, Magnetic tape, Floppy, CD

(b) CD, DVD, Magnetic tape, Floppy

(c) Floppy, CD, DVD, Magnetic tape

(d) Magnetic tape, Floppy, CD, DVD

28. Identify the correct order of evolution of computers:
    (a) PC-XT, PC-AT, Main frame, Micro
    (b) PC-AT, PC-XT, Main frame, Micro
    (c) Micro, PC-AT, PC-XT, Main frame
    (d) Main frame, Micro, PC-AT, PC-XT
29. Identify the correct order of evolution of the following storage order
    (a) Paper, Micro card, Magnetic tape, Clay tablet
    (b) Clay tablet, Paper, Micro card, Magnetic tape
    (c) Micro card, Magnetic tape, Clay tablet, Paper
    (d) Magnetic tape, Clay tablet, Paper, Micro card
30. Identify the correct chronological order in which the following were established:
    (a) **National Library of India (Kolkata)**(1948), **Delhi Public Library** (1950), **Documentation Research and Training Centre** (1962), **Raja Ram Mohan Roy Library Foundation** (1972)
    (b) Delhi Public Library, Documentation Research and Training Centre, Raja Ram Mohan Roy Library Foundation , National Library of India (Kolkata)
    (c) Documentation Research and Training Centre, Raja Ram Mohan Roy Library Foundation, National Library of India (Kolkata), Delhi Public Library
    (d) Raja Ram Mohan Roy Library Foundation, National Library of India (Kolkata), Delhi Public Library, Documentation Research and Training Centre
31. Which one of the sequences is in ascending order?
    (a) Bytes, Gigabytes, Megabytes, Terrabytes
    (b) Bytes (8 bits), Megabytes (2^{10}bytes/10^3 bytes), Gigabytes (2^{20} bytes/10^6 bytes), Terrabytes (2^{40} bytes/10^{12} bytes)
    (c) Bytes, Terrabytes, Megabytes, Gigabytes
    (d) Megabytes, Bytes, Terrabytes, Gigabytes
32. Which of the following would be the correct chronological sequence?
    (a) Bibliometrics, Informetrics, Librametry, Webometrics

(b) Librametry, Bibliommetrics, Informetrics, Webometrics

(c) Librametry, Informetrics, Bibliometrics, Webometrics

(d) Bibliometrics, Informetrics, Webometrics, Librametry

33. Arrange the physical forms of catalogue in the chronological sequence:

(a) Register, Sheaf Catalogue, Card Catalogue, OPAC

(b) Sheaf Catalogue, Register, Card Catalogue, OPAC

(c) Card Catalogue, Sheaf Catalogue, Register, OPAC

(d) Sheaf Catalogue, Card Catalogue, Register, OPAC

34. Match the following:

	List-I (Term)	**List-II (Forms of Communication)**
(a)	Invisible college	(i) Physical carrier
(b)	Noise	(ii) Formal channel
(c)	Medium	(iii) Barrier
(d)	Document	(iv) Informal channel

Codes:

	(a)	(b)	(c)	(d)
(a)	(i)	(ii)	(iii)	(iv)
(b)	(ii)	(i)	(iii)	(iv)
(c)	(iv)	(iii)	(ii)	(i)
(d)	**(iv)**	**(iii)**	**(i)**	**(ii)**

35. Match the following:

	List-I (Work)	**List-II (Author)**
(a)	Subject Classification	(i) J.Atchinson
(b)	Thesaurofacet	(ii) C.A.Cutter
(c)	Classified Catalogue Code	(iii) J.D.Brown
(d)	Rules for Dictionary Catalogue	(iv) S.R.Ranganathan

Codes:

	(a)	(b)	(c)	(d)
(a)	**(iii)**	**(i)**	**(iv)**	**(ii)**
(b)	(ii)	(iii)	(i)	(iv)
(c)	(iv)	(ii)	(iii)	(i)
(d)	(i)	(ii)	(iii)	(iv)

36. Match the following:

	List-I (Research Methods)	**List-II (Type)**
(a)	Content analysis	(i) Data Collection Tool
(b)	Questionnaire	(ii) Qualitative Methods of Analysis
(c)	Observation	(iii) Methods of Research
(d)	Case Study	(iv) Direct Method

Codes:

	(a)	(b)	(c)	(d)
(a)	(i)	(iv)	(iii)	(ii)
(b)	**(ii)**	**(i)**	**(iv)**	**(iii)**
(c)	(iii)	(ii)	(i)	(iv)
(d)	(iv)	(iii)	(ii)	(i)

37. Match the following:

	List-I	**List-II**
(a)	Maharashtra Public Libraries Act	(i) 2004
(b)	Gujarat Public Libraries Act	(ii) 2005
(c)	Orissa Public Libraries Act	(iii) 1967
(d)	West Bengal Public Libraries Act	(iv) 1988
		(v) 1979

Codes:

	(a)	(b)	(c)	(d)
(a)	(i)	(iii)	(ii)	(iv)
(b)	(ii)	(v)	(iv)	(iii)
(c)	**(iii)**	**(i)**	**(ii)**	**(v)**
(d)	(v)	(ii)	(iv)	(iii)

38. Match the following:

	List-I	**List-II**
(a)	Scientific Management	(i) Esprit de crops
(b)	Unity of Command	(ii) Peter Drucker
(c)	Management by Objectives	(iii) Factor of Planning
(d)	Forecasting	(iv) Efficiency and Waste Prevention

Codes:

	(a)	(b)	(c)	(d)
(a)	**(iv)**	**(i)**	**(ii)**	**(iii)**
(b)	(i)	(ii)	(iii)	(iv)
(c)	(ii)	(iii)	(i)	(iv)
(d)	(iii)	(i)	(iv)	(ii)

39. Match the following:

	List-I	**List-II**
(a)	Search Engine	(i) Internet Explorer
(b)	Subject Gateway	(ii) Dogpile
(c)	Net Browser	(iii) FTP
(d)	Meta Search Engine	(iv) SOSIG
		(v) Altavista

Codes:

	(a)	(b)	(c)	(d)
(a)	(iv)	(iii)	(ii)	(i)
(b)	**(v)**	**(iv)**	**(i)**	**(ii)**
(c)	(v)	(i)	(ii)	(iii)
(d)	(v)	(i)	(iv)	(ii)

40. Match the following:

	List-I	**List-II**
(a)	ERNET	(i) Japan
(b)	JANET	(ii) Global
(c)	RLIN	(iii) India
(d)	OCLC	(iv) United Kingdom
		(v) USA

Codes:

	(a)	(b)	(c)	(d)
(a)	(v)	(iv)	(i)	(iii)
(b)	(iv)	(v)	(i)	(ii)
(c)	**(iii)**	**(iv)**	**(v)**	**(ii)**
(d)	(iii)	(ii)	(iv)	(v)

41. Match the the following:

	List-I	List-II
(a)	Origin of a word	(i) World of Learning
(b)	Synonyms for a word	(ii) Dictionary of Etymology
(c)	How to install a gadget	(iii) Encyclopedia
(d)	Address of Oxford University	(iv) Manual
		(v) Thesaurus

Codes:

	(a)	(b)	(c)	(d)
(a)	(ii)	(v)	(iv)	(iii)
(b)	(v)	(iii)	(iv)	(i)
(c)	(v)	(iv)	(i)	(iii)
(d)	**(ii)**	**(v)**	**(iv)**	**(i)**

42. Match the following:

	List-I	List-II
(a)	Nehru Memorial Museum Library	(i) Chennai
(b)	Connemara Public Library	(ii) Pune
(c)	Bhandkar Oriental Research Institute Library	(iii) Patna
(d)	Khudabaksh Oriental Library	(iv) Delhi
		(v) Allahabad

Codes:

	(a)	(b)	(c)	(d)
(a)	(iii)	(v)	(iv)	(ii)
(b)	(v)	(iv)	(i)	(ii)
(c)	(v)	(ii)	(iv)	(i)
(d)	**(iv)**	**(i)**	**(ii)**	**(iii)**

43. Match the following:

	List-I	**List-II**
(a)	IFLA	(i) Science Citation Index
(b)	UNESCO	(ii) First serach
(c)	OCLC	(iii) Patent information
(d)	ISI	(iv) Public Library Manifesto
		(v) Universal Availability of Publications

Codes:

	(a)	(b)	(c)	(d)
(a)	(iii)	(iv)	(ii)	(i)
(b)	(iv)	(iii)	(i)	(ii)
(c)	**(v)**	**(iv)**	**(ii)**	**(i)**
(d)	(v)	(i)	(iv)	(ii)

44. Match the following:

	List-I	**List-II**
(a)	E-Mail	(i) Bulletin Board
(b)	FTP	(ii) Remote Log In
(c)	TELNET	(iii) Library Network
(d)	USENET	(iv) Moving/Downloading Files
		(v) Exchanging Message

Codes:

	(a)	(b)	(c)	(d)
(a)	(iv)	(iii)	(v)	(i)
(b)	**(v)**	**(iv)**	**(ii)**	**(i)**
(c)	(ii)	(iv)	(i)	(iii)
(d)	(v)	(i)	(iv)	(iii)

45. Match the following:

	List-I	**List-II**
(a)	MS-DOS	(i) Multi-User Operating System
(b)	UNIX	(ii) DTP Software
(c)	Excel	(iii) DBMS
(d)	pagemaker	(iv) Single User Operating System
		(v) Spreadsheet Software

Codes:

	(a)	(b)	(c)	(d)
(a)	(iv)	(v)	(i)	(ii)
(b)	(v)	(i)	(ii)	(iii)
(c)	(iii)	(i)	(ii)	(v)
(d)	**(iv)**	**(i)**	**(v)**	**(ii)**

COMPREHENSION TEST:

46. The distinguishing features of digital devices are:
    (i) Speed (ii) Accuracy
    (iii) Timeliness (iv) Easy to Carry
    (a) (i) and (ii) (b) (ii) and (iv)
    (c) (iv), (iii) and (i) (d) (ii), (iii) and (iv)
47. Digital clocks are analog in nature because:
    (a) they have two hands
    (b) their hands sweep along on a continuous scale
    (c) they show time
    (d) display discrete numbers standing for time
48. Hybrid computers are developed to take advantage of:
    (a) strength of analog devices
    (b) strength of digital devices
    (c) strength of both analog and digital devices
    (d) strength of none of the above
49. Analog computers measure physical quantities because of:
    (a) the temperature and accuracy
    (b) their greater speed and accuracy
    (c) the human beings
    (d) the complexities in operations
50. Digital computers assume more importance in applied information science because
    (a) The lack of capabilities for symbol manipulation
    (b) the capabilities for symbol manipulation
    (c) the capabilities for digital manipulation
    (d) the lack of capabilities for digital manipulation

June 2007

1. Fundamental facts of research are available in

   (a) Primary sources (b) Secondary sources

   (c) Tertiary sources (d) None of the above

2. POSDCORB coined by:

   (a) Fayol (b) Maslow

   (c) Gulick (d) Ranganathan

3. OCLC Project, MARC Project are the examples of:

   (a) Co-operative storage of materials

   (b) Co-operative acquisition of materials

   (c) Co-operative processing of materials

   (d) Co-operative stharing of materials

4. Peter Phyrr developed this technique:

   (a) PPBS (b) Line by Line Budget

   (c) Zero Based Budgeting(d) Performance Budget

5. The unit of measuring the speed of the transmission of the data is called:

   (a) Band (b) Protocol

   (c) HTTP (d) RAM

6. Dublin core is related to:

   (a) Metadata (b) MARC

   (c) ISBD (d) CCF

7. "God has chosen me as an instrument, the honour done to me should act as an incentive to the younger generation to devote their lives whole heartedly to library science and service". Whose quotation is this?

   (a) B.S.Kesavan (b) Melvil Dewey

   (c) S.R.Ranganathan (d) W.C.B.Sayers

8. Routing of periodicals is considered as:

   (a) CAS (b) SDI

   (c) Translation service

   (d) Indexing and Abstracting service

9. A statement that is to be tested in research is called:

   (a) Problem (b) Assumption

   (c) Hypothesis (d) All the above

10. ISDN stands for:
    (a) International Standard Digital Network
    (b) International Standard Distributed Network
    (c) Integrated Services Digital Network
    (d) Integrated Services Distributed Network
11. The following is the search engine for scientific information only:
    (a) Google **(b) SCIRUS**
    (c) Yahoo (d) Alta Vista
12. One of the following has designed models of communication:
    (a) Shannon and Weaver
    (b) Ranganathan and Neelameghan
    (c) Losswell and Gerbher
    (d) Blake and Mouton
13. OAI stands for:
    (a) Open Access Initiatives
    (b) Open Archives Initiatives
    (c) On-line Archives Initiatives
    (d) On-line Access Initiatives
14. Maslow's theory is related to:
    (a) Motivation (b) Leadership
    (c) Maturity (d) Scientific management
15. CALIBER is sponsored by:
    (a) INFLIBNET (b) DELNET
    (c) AGRINET (d) CALIBNET
16. Headquarters of UNESCO
    (a) Washington **(b) Paris**
    (c) London (d) The Hague
17. "Search strategy is the mirror in the dark". Whose quotation is this?
    (a) Kartz (b) Ranganathan
    (c) Bliss (d) Cutter
18. INDEST is a
    (a) Bibliography **(b) Consortium**
    (c) Directory (d) Dictionary

19. ISBN now consists of
    (a) 10 digits **(b) 13 digits**
    (c) 15 digits (d) 8 digits
20. Which Association was estanlished in 1876?
    (a) LA **(b) ALA**
    (c) ILA (d) IASLIC
21. Encyclopaedia of library and information science is published by:
    (a) H.W.Wilson (b) R.R.Bowker
    (c) Marcel Dekker (d) Andrew Deutsch
22. This particular law of library science gives emphasis on the delegation of the government to enact library legislation in their respective states:
    (a) First Law **(b) Second Law**
    (c) Third Law (d) Fourth Law
23. **Assertion (a):** Research is a total process consisting of a series of steps.
    Reason (R): Sometimes several steps are carried out simultaneously.
    Codes:
    (a) Both (a) and (R) are True
    (b) Both (a) and (R) are False
    (c) (a) is true and (R) is false
    (d) (R) is True and (a) is False
24. **Assertion (a) :** Now a days marketing of information products is necessity.
    Reason (R) : Information is an important source.
    Codes:
    (a) (a) is True but (R) is False
    (b) (a) is False but (R) is True
    (c) Both (a) and (R) are True
    (d) Both (a) and (R) are False
25. **Assertion (a):** Internet is an important tool for the dissemination of information.
    Reason (R): Large number of open sources are available

Codes:

(a) (a) is True but (R) is False

(b) (a) is False but (R) is True

(c) Both (a) and (R) are True

(d) Both (a) and (R) are False

26. **Assertion (a) :** Libraries of tomorrow will become more information service oriented centres.

Reason (R): They would require more powerful tools for storage and retrieval of information.

Codes:

(a) **Both (a) and (R) are True and (R) is the correct explanation of (a)**

(b) Both (a) and (R) are True but (R) is not the correct explanation of (a)

(c) (a) is True but (R) is False

(d) (a) is False but (R) is True

27. **Assertion (a):** Training programme for library and information professionals can be developed on the lines of proportional education and continuing education.

Reason (R): Continuing education programme must take care of information demands of the clientele of the parent organisation from time to time.

Codes:

(a) Both (a) and (R) are True, but (R) is not the correct explanation of (a)

(b) Both (a) and (R) are False

(c) (a) is False and (R) is True

(d) (a) is True and (R) is False

28. **Assertion (a):** Dewey Decmal Classification is popularly used in libraries with large collections.

Reason (R) : It is being regularly updated.

Codes:

(a) (a) is True but (R) is False

(b) (a) is False but (R) is True

(c) Both (a) and (R) are False

(d) Both (a) and (R) are True

29. **Assertion (a) :** Book selection must be done judiciously.

Reason (R) : Resource sharing is the need of the day.

Codes:

(a) Both (a) and (R) True and (R) is the correct explanation of (a)

(b) Both (a) and (R) are False.

(c) Both (a) and (R) are True but (R) is not the correct explanation of (a).

(d) (a) is False but (R) is True.

30. Arrange the following in the chronological sequence of their development.

(i) Pascal (1970) (ii) Cobol (1959)

(iii) Fortran (1957) (iv) Basic (1979)

Codes:

(a) (i) (ii) (iv) (iii) **(b) (iii) (ii) (i) (iv)**

(c) (ii) (iv) (iii) (i) (d) (iii) (iv) (ii) (i)

31. Arrange the following catalogue codes according to the year of publication.

(i) Classified catalogue code (ii) AA code

(iii) AACR II (iv) RDC

Codes:

(a) (i) (iii) (ii) (iv) **(b) (iv) (ii) (i) (iii)**

(c) (ii) (iii) (i) (iv) (d) (i) (iv) (iii) (ii)

32. Arrange the following according to the work flow:

(a) Dissemination, Selection, Processing, Acquisition

(b) Selection, Processing, Acquisition, Dissemination

(c) Selection, Acquisition, Processing, Dissemination

(d) Processing, Acquisition, Dissemination, Selection

33. Arrange the following according to the preferred order of sources for information

(i) Colophon | (ii) Outside the issue
(iii) Title Page | (iv) Preface

Codes:

(a) (i) (ii) (iv) (iii) | (b) (ii) (iii) (iv) (i)
(c) (iii) (i) (iv) (ii) | (d) (i) (iii) (iv) (ii)

34. Identify the correct chronological order in which they were set up:

(a) ILA, IASLIC, APLA, IATLIS
(b) APLA, ILA, IASLIC, IATLIS
(c) IASLIC, ILA, IATLIS, APLA
(d) IATLIS, IASLIC, ILA, APLA

35. Match the following:

List-I	**List-II**
(a) Pre-Scientific Period	(i) Pre 1927
(b) Scientific Period	(ii) Pre 1880
(c) Human Relations	(iii) 1880-1927
(d) Synthesis	(iv) 1927-1950
	(v) 1950-2007

Codes:

	(a)	(b)	(c)	(d)
(a)	(i)	(ii)	(iv)	(v)
(b)	**(ii)**	**(iii)**	**(iv)**	**(v)**
(c)	(iii)	(iv)	(v)	(ii)
(d)	(ii)	(iii)	(v)	(iv)

36. Match the following:

List-I	**List-II**
(a) OCLC	(i) City
(b) INFLIBNET	(ii) International
(c) CALIBNET	(iii) Regional
(d) ASTINFO	(iv) National

Codes:

	(a)	(b)	(c)	(d)
(a)	(ii)	(i)	(iv)	(iii)

(b)	**(ii)**	**(iv)**	**(i)**	**(iii)**
(c)	(iii)	(ii)	(iv)	(i)
(d)	(iii)	(i)	(ii)	(iv)

37. Match the following:

List-I	**List-II**
(a) Biological Abstracts	(i) H.W.Wilson
(b) Statesman Yearbook	(ii) NISCAIR
(c) Indian Science Abstracts	(iii) Institute of Scientific Information
(d) Cumulative Book List	(iv)U N Statistical Office

Codes:

	(a)	(b)	(c)	(d)
(a)	(i)	(iii)	(iv)	(ii)
(b)	**(iii)**	**(iv)**	**(ii)**	**(i)**
(c)	(iv)	(ii)	(iii)	(i)
(d)	(ii)	(iii)	(i)	(iv)

38. Match the following:

List-I	**List-II**
(a) B.S.Kesavan	(i) Cataloguing Rules
(b) W.C.B.Sayers	(ii) National Library
(c) C.A.Cutter	(iii) School of Librarianship
(d) J.D.Brown	(iv) List of Subject Headings
	(v) Subject Classification

Codes:

	(a)	(b)	(c)	(d)
(a)	(v)	(iii)	(ii)	(i)
(b)	(iii)	(ii)	(iv)	(v)
(c)	**(ii)**	**(iii)**	**(i)**	**(v)**
(d)	(v)	(ii)	(iv)	(i)

39. Match the following:

List-I	**List-II**
(a) NISCAIR	(i) MINISIS
(b) DESIDOC	(ii) LibSys
(c) IDRC	(iii) Granthalaya
(d) INFOTEK	(iv) Sanjay
	(v) SLIM

Codes:

	(a)	(b)	(c)	(d)
(a)	(ii)	(v)	(iii)	(iv)
(b)	(i)	(ii)	(v)	(iv)
(c)	(iii)	(ii)	(i)	(v)
(d)	**(iii)**	**(iv)**	**(i)**	**(ii)**

40. Match the following:

List-I	**List-II**
(a) Journal of Librarianship	(i) Delhi
(b) Herald of Library Science	(ii)London
(c) Library Herald	(iii)New York
(d) Library Literature	(iv)Lucknow
	(v) Canada

Codes:

	(a)	(b)	(c)	(d)
(a)	(ii)	(iv)	(i)	(iii)
(b)	(iv)	(iii)	(i)	(v)
(c)	(iii)	(ii)	(v)	(iv)
(d)	**(ii)**	**(i)**	**(iv)**	**(iii)**

41. Match the following:

List-I	**List-II**
(a) Blake	(i) Chart technique
(b) Gantt	(ii) Leadership Style
(c) Maslow	(iii)Maturity/Immaturity theory
(d) McGregor	(iv) Motivation Theory
	(v) Theory X and Y

Codes:

	(a)	(b)	(c)	(d)
(a)	(ii)	(iii)	(v)	(iv)
(b)	**(ii)**	**(i)**	**(iv)**	**(v)**
(c)	(iii)	(iv)	(ii)	(i)
(d)	(i)	(iv)	(iii)	(ii)

42. Match the following:

List-I	**List-II**
(a) INIS	(i) 1950

(b) AGRIS	(ii) 1970
(c) INPADOC	(iii) 1972
(d) OCLC	(iv) 1974
	(v) 1967

Codes:

	(a)	(b)	(c)	(d)
(a)	(iv)	(iii)	(ii)	(v)
(b)	**(ii)**	**(iv)**	**(iii)**	**(v)**
(c)	(i)	(iv)	(ii)	(iii)
(d)	(ii)	(iii)	(v)	(iv)

43. Match the following:

List-I	**List-II**
(a) Search Engine	(i) PASCAL
(b) Browser	(ii) UNIX
(c) Operating System	(iii) Yahoo
(d) Programming Language	(iv) Netscape
	(v) HTTP

Codes:

	(a)	(b)	(c)	(d)
(a)	(i)	(iv)	(v)	(ii)
(b)	(iv)	(iii)	(ii)	(i)
(c)	**(iii)**	**(iv)**	**(ii)**	**(i)**
(d)	(iv)	(ii)	(i)	(v)

44. Match the following:

List-I	**List-II**
(a) Pre-natal Cataloguing	(i) Shared Cataloguing Programme
(b) NPAC	(ii) Library of Congress
(c) CIP	(iii) NUCSSI
(d) Union Catalogue	(iv) S.R.Ranganthan

Codes:

	(a)	**(b)**	**(c)**	**(d)**
(a)	(iii)	(ii)	(i)	(iv)
(b)	**(iv)**	**(i)**	**(ii)**	**(iii)**
(c)	(i)	(iv)	(iii)	(ii)
(d)	(ii)	(iii)	(i)	(iv)

45. Match the following:

List-I	List-II
(a) Subject indexing	(i) P.M.Rogget
(b) Keyword indexing	(ii) H.P.Luhn
(c) Automated indexing	(iii)H.Ohlman
(d) SLIC indexing	(iv)M.E.Sears
	(v) S.L.McNold

Codes:

	(a)	(b)	(c)	(d)
(a)	(iii)	(ii)	(iv)	(i)
(b)	**(iv)**	**(i)**	**(ii)**	**(iii)**
(c)	(ii)	(i)	(v)	(iv)
(d)	(v)	(iii)	(iv)	(ii)

COMPREHENSION TEST

46. Now a days much thought is given for:
(a) Curriculum requirements
(b) Broad based education
(c) Information scientists
(d) All the above

47. India cannot afford to neglect the aspects of manpower training because:
(a) of proliferation of library schools
(b) of in-sufficient provision of library schools
(c) they are crucial to the success of development
(d) they are not crucial for the success of development

48. Specialized information science education institutes produce better professionals as:
(a) library schools fail to produce good professionals
(b) library schools are unable to meet the demands of the society
(c) **they have better curricula and infrastructure**
(d) they do not have good curricula

49. LIS education is now pertinent to:
(a) design curricula
(b) follow existing curricula

(c) have status quo in curricula
(d) reduce the curricula

50. Training for librarianship must be at par:
(a) with the old set up
(b) with the future set up
(c) with the present set up
(d) with the previous set up

December 2007

1. These documents are not primary sources:
(a) Thesis (b) Patents
(c) Conference Papers **(d) Reference Books**

2. World of Learning is:
(a) A Bibliography (b) An Abstract
(c) An Encyclopaedia **(d) A Directory**

3. Headquarters of IFLA is located in:
(a) Paris (b) Washington
(c) London **(d) The Haque**

4. National Library for visual handicapped is situated in:
(a) Mumbai (b) Mysore
(c) New Delhi **(d) Dehradun**

5. The first page of Website is known as:
(a) Cover Page **(b) Home Page**
(c) Title Page (d) Half Title Page

6. Blog is a:
(a) Off-line Journal (b) Internet Journal
(c) Web Directory (d) Search Engine

7. This literature is not published and not available through normal book selling channels
(a) Grey Literature (b) Text Books
(c) Journals (d) None of the above

8. The owner of Internet is:
(a) American Mathematical Society
(b) Department of Science and Technology, Govt. of India

(c) British Standard Institute

(d) None of the above

9. Library as a living system "takes a new matter, casts off old matter, changes in size and takes new shapes and term". Whose quotation is this?

(a) B.S.Kesavan (b) Melvil Dewey

(c) S.R.Ranganathan (d) W.C.B.Sayers

10. Handling of Information in the sense of production is called:

(a) Information marketing

(b) Information Industry

(c) Information Production

(d) Information Revolution

11. SCOPUS is a:

(a) Full Text Database

(b) Abstracts and Citation Database

(c) Numerical Database

(d) None of the above

12. "Choice of books is an unending work" whose quotation is this?

(a) Melvil Dewey (b) W.C.B.Sayers

(c) C.A.Cutter (d) H.E.Bliss

13. Which of the following is not an Open Source Software?

(a) Green Stone (b) D-Space

(c) Plone **(d) Delmark**

14. NACLIN is sponsored by:

(a) INFLIBNET **(b) DELNET**

(c) AGRINET (d) CALIBNET

15. The latest State, which enacted Public Libraries Act is:

(a) **Bihar** (b) Uttaranchal

(c) Uttar Pradesh (d) Orissa

16. UNISIST, a project of UNESCO was launched in this year:

(a) 1994 **(b) 1972**

(c) 1958 (d) 2001

17. The term "Information Science" came into existence in this year:

(a) 1988 **(b) 1959**
(c) 1961 (d) 1975

18. 'Dublin Core Metadata' consists of:

(a) 11 elements (b) 13 elements
(c) 10 elements **(d) 15 elements**

19. System school of management is based on the contribution of:

(a) Taylor (b) Gilberts
(c) Fayol **(d) Urwick**

20. "The high purpose of Book Selection is to provide the right reader at the right time". Whose quotation is this?

(a) Francis Drury (b) H.E.Bliss
(c) Melvil Dewey (d) C.A.Cutter

21. "The Wheat loan Educational Exchange Programme" was initiated in:

(a) 1951 (b) 1972
(c) 1981 (d) 1999

22. Weeding of unuseful books from the library is emphasized by this law of library science:

(a) Second (b) Third
(c) Fourth **(d) Fifth**

23. **Assertion (A)**: In survey research, the commonly used techniques for gathering data are questionnaire, the interview and the observational techniques.

Reason (R) : These are least effective for collecting data about perceptions, beliefs, attitudes, etc. of persons

Codes:

(a) (A) is true and (R) is false
(b) (A) is false and (R) is true
(c) Both (A) and (R) are true
(d) Both (A) and (R) are false.

24. **Assertion (A) :** Information is a resource whose generation consumes time and money.

Reason (R) : Information is a resource where we consume time and money.

Codes:

(a) Both (A) and (R) are true but (R) is not the right explanation of (A)

(b) **Both (A) and (R) are true and (R) is the right explanation of (A)**

(d) (A) is true but (R) is false

(d) (A) is false but (R) is true

25. **Assertion (A):** Information literacy is necessary for the users.

Reason (R): It promotes the use of libraries and information centres.

Codes:

(a) Both (A) and (R) are true

(b) Both (A) and (R) are false

(c) (A) is true but (R) is false

(d) (a) is false but (R) is true

26. **Assertion (A):** Evaluation of information is necessary.

Reason (R): Anybody can write on internet.

Codes:

(a) Both (A) and (R) are false

(b) Both (A) and (R) are true

(c) (A) is true but (R) is false

(d) (A) is false but (R) is true

27. **Assertion (A):** Libraries have no scope for the growth and development in future.

Reason (R): E-resources can be used anywhere anytime.

Codes:

(a) Both (A) and (R) are true

(b) Both (A) and (R) are false

(c) (A) is false but (R) is true

(d) (A) is true but (R) is false

28. **Assertion (A):** Several methods can be devised for assisting librarians to keep abreast of developments in his field to maintain efficiency.

Reason (R): Seminars, conferences, workshops can solve the purpose.

Codes:

(a) Both (A) and (R) are true but (R) is not the correct explanation of (A)

(b) Both (A) and (R) are true and (R) is the correct expression of (A).

(c) (A) is true but (R) is false

(d) (A) is false but (R) is true

29. **Assertion (A):** Stock verification is essential in the collection development for libraries.

Reason (R): It is a time consuming process.

Codes:

(a) (A) is true but (R) is false

(b) Both (A) and (R) are true but (R) is not the right explanation of (a).

(c) Both (A) and (R) are true and (R) is the right explanation of (A)

(d) Both (A) and (R) are false

30. **Assertion (A):** Organization chart can be a useful management tool.

Reason (R): It gives clear picture of the formal lines of communication within the library.

Codes:

(a) (A) is true but (R) is false

(b) (A) is false but (R) is true

(c) Both (A) and (R) are true

(d) Both (A) and (R) are false

31. **Assertion (A) :** ISBD (S) is concerned with the serial publications.

Reason (R): It is not used for the serials which have ceased their publication.

Codes:

(a) (A) is true but (R) is false

(b) (A) is false but (R) is true

(c) Both (A) and (R) are true

(d) Both (A) and (R) are false

32. Arrange the following research steps according to the sequence of their occurrence

(i) Formulation of hypothesis of research

(ii) Designing of data and analysis plan

(iii) Selection of data gathering method

(iv) Report writing

Codes:

(a) (iii), (ii), (i), (iv) **(b) (i), (iii), (ii), (iv)**

(c) (iii), (i), (iv), (ii) (d) (ii), (iv), (i), (ii)

33. Identify the development in the following library softwares in correct chronological sequence.

Codes:

(a) CDS/ISIS, SOUL, Green Stone, DSpace

(b) DSpace, SOUL, CDS/ISIS, Green Stone

(c) Green Stone, CDS/ISIS, DSpace, SOUL

(d) SOUL, DSpace, Green Stone, CDS/ISIS

34. Identify the chronological order of the following Public Libraries Acts.

(i) Andhra Pradesh Public Libraries Act

(ii) Karnataka Public libraries Act

(iii) Haryana Public Libraries Act

(iv) Maharashtra Public Libraries Act

Codes:

(a) (ii), (iv), (iii), (i) **(b) (i), (ii), (iv), (iii)**

(c) (iii), (ii), (i), (iv) (d) (iv), (iii), (i), (ii)

35. Identify the chronological order of the following Cataloguing Codes:

(i) AACR II (ii) CCC

(iii) AA Code (iv) ALA code

Codes:

(a) (iii), (iv), (i), (ii) (b) (ii), (iv), (iii), (i)

(c) (iii), (ii), (iv), (i) (d) (iv), (i), (ii), (iii)

36. (i) Arrange the following in chronological order of their origin:

(i) Unix (ii) MS-DOS

(iii) Linux (iv) Windows

Codes:

(a) (iv), (ii), (iii), (i) **(b) (ii), (i), (iv), (iii)**

(c) (i), (iii), (iv), (ii) (d) (iii), (i), (iv), (ii)

37. Identify the correct chronological order in which the following networks were launched.

(i) NICNET (ii) ERNET

(iii) DELNET (iv) INDONET

Codes:

(a) (iii), (iv), (ii), (i) (b) (i), (iii), (iv), (ii)

(c) (ii), (i), (iii), (iv) (d) (iv), (iii), (i), (ii)

38. Arrange the following management developments chronologically:

(i) Synthesis Period (ii) Scientific Period

(iii) Human Relation (iv) Pre-Scientific Period

Codes:

(a) (iii), (i), (ii), (iv) **(b) (iv), (ii), (iii), (i)**

(c) (i), (iv), (ii), (iii) (d) (ii), (i), (iv), (iii)

39. Match the following:

List-I	**List-II**
(a) Simplex	(i) Communication channel is used in both the directions but only in one direction at a time
(b) Half Duplex	(ii) Communication channel is used in one direction
(c) Full Duplex	(iii) Bits of information are transmitted continuously
(d) Asynchronous transmission	(iv) Information is sent at random intervals with

start and stop bits for each batch of information

Codes:

	(a)	(b)	(c)	(d)
(a)	(ii)	(i)	(iv)	(iii)
(b)	(i)	(iv)	(iii)	(ii)
(c)	**(iv)**	**(ii)**	**(i)**	**(iii)**
(d)	(iv)	(i)	(iii)	(ii)

40. Match the following:

List-I	**List-II**
(a) Taylor	(i) Theory of Motivation
(b) Maslow	(ii) X and Y Theory
(c) McGregor	(iii) Scientific Management
(d) Argyris	(iv) Immaturity/Maturity Theory
	(v) Leadership Style

Codes:

	(a)	(b)	(c)	(d)
(a)	(iii)	(iv)	(ii)	(i)
(b)	(iv)	(i)	(v)	(iii)
(c)	**(iii)**	**(i)**	**(ii)**	**(iv)**
(d)	(v)	(iv)	(iii)	(i)

41. Match the following:

List-I	**List-II**
(a) SOUL	(i) INFOTEK
(b) LIBSYS	(ii) ALGORITHM
(c) SLIM	(iii) UNESCO
(d) WINISIS	(iv) INFLIBNET
	(v) DESIDOC

Codes:

	(a)	(b)	(c)	(d)
(a)	(iii)	(v)	(iv)	(i)
(b)	**(iv)**	**(i)**	**(ii)**	**(iii)**
(c)	(v)	(iv)	(i)	(iii)
(d)	(i)	(iii)	(v)	(ii)

42. Match the following:

List-I	**List-II**
(a) Fyzee Committeee	(i) Library Budget
(b) Knowledge Commission	(ii) Status and Payscales of libraries
(c) Mahrotra Committee	(iii) Public Libraries
(d) Kothari Commission	(iv) Knowledge Society
	(v) Importance of library in academic institutions

Codes:

	(a)	(b)	(c)	(d)
(a)	(i)	(iv)	(iii)	(v)
(b)	(iv)	(ii)	(v)	(iii)
(c)	(v)	(ii)	(iv)	(iii)
(d)	**(iii)**	**(iv)**	**(ii)**	**(i)**

43. Match the following:

List-I	**List-II**
(a) Protocol	(i) Java
(b) Language	(ii) Internet Explorer
(c) Browser	(iii) Altavista
(d) Search Engine	(iv) DOS
	(v) HTTP

Codes:

	(a)	(b)	(c)	(d)
(a)	(iv)	(v)	(i)	(iii)
(b)	**(v)**	**(i)**	**(ii)**	**(iii)**
(c)	(ii)	(iv)	(v)	(i)
(d)	(i)	(v)	(iv)	(ii)

44. Match the following:

List-I	**List-II**
(a) INIS	(i) Institute of Electrical Engineering, UK
(b) AGRIS	(ii) International Atomic Energy Agency, Vienna
(c) MEDLINE	(iii) Agricultural Organization of UN, Rome

(d) INSPEC (iv) National Library of Medicine, USA

Codes:

	(a)	(b)	(c)	(d)
(a)	(iii)	(ii)	(i)	(iv)
(b)	**(ii)**	**(iii)**	**(iv)**	**(i)**
(c)	(iv)	(ii)	(iii)	(i)
(d)	(ii)	(i)	(iii)	(iv)

45. Match the following:

List-I	**List-II**
(a) Paul Otlet	(i) List of Subject Heading
(b) Fermont Rider	(ii) Role operators
(c) George Boole	(iii) National Library
(d) Minie Sears	(iv) International Classification
	(v) Universal Decimal Classification

Codes:

	(a)	(b)	(c)	(d)
(a)	(iii)	(i)	(v)	(iv)
(b)	**(v)**	**(iv)**	**(ii)**	**(i)**
(c)	(iv)	(v)	(i)	(ii)
(d)	(i)	(iv)	(iii)	(v)

46. Industrial environment in India is making a quantum jump because:

(a) Information is a resource whose generation consumes time

(b) Information is a resource whose generation is money

(c) Information is a resource that consumes money and time

(d) Information absorptions and innovation in the field of the technology

47. Monopoly in business is coming to an end because of a:

(a) Information (b) Money flow

(c) Competitiveness (d) Lack of information

48. Information is a major resource which:

(a) helps company to lose money

(b) helps company to have an edge in competition

(d) helps company to gain better manpower

49. Electronics industry is both an important and competent industry as it:

(a) is growing at the rate of fifteen percent

(b) is growing at the rate of five hundred percent

(c) is growing at the rate of fourteen percent

(d) is not growing at all

50. The types of information usually sought by companies are:

(a) economic and legal information

(b) information on personnel relation

(c) information on technology and market trends

(d) all the above

June 2008

1. Who is the Chairman of National Knowledge Commission?

(a) Harsha Parekh (b) P.B.Mangla

(c) Kalpana Dasgupta **(d) Sam Pitroda**

2. Who has not change its name?

(a) Library Association, U.K. **(b) ALA**

(c) ASLIB (d) IFLA

3. Which of the following is not correct?

(a) Maslow's need analysis is useful for understanding motivation of employees.

(b) **Theory Z is the contribution of Japanese style of Management.**

(c) Money is the most powerful motivating agent.

(d) Mission of an organization is essentially abstract.

4. NISCAIR is a part of:

(a) DST (b) ISRO

(c) DSIR **(d) CSIR**

5. Use of Microfilming is considerably reduced due to:

(a) Problems of preservation of microfilming

(b) Need for use microfilm reader

(c) Availability of better technology in the form of digitization

(d) High cost involved in it.

6. Opaque paper is a:

(a) Ultra-white paper (b) Ultra-white thin paper

(c) Transparent paper **(d) Non-Transparent paper**

7. Which of the following is a public domain database:

(a) INIS **(b) AGRIS**

(c) Chemical Abstracts (d) MEDLINE

8. In which Library Service barcode technology is used:

(a) Stock verification (b) Library security

(c) Circulation (d) Reference service

9. One of the following journal is published in UK:

(a) Library Quarterly **(b) Program**

(c) Libri (d) Herald of Library Science

10. 'Fair use' is a term most relevant to:

(a) Intellectual Property Rights

(b) Books borrowed for home reading

(c) Copyright

(d) Use of reference books

11. Which of the following does not fall into the category of pre-coordinate indexing

(a) Chain indexing

(b) Uniform indexing

(c) LCSH

(d) Sear's List of Subject Headings

12. Dublin core is:

(a) A set of core activities of a National Library

(b) Collection of metadata elements

(c) Network for the city of Dublin

(d) Revised version of MARC

13. 'Best is the enemy of the Good' is said by:

(a) Drury **(b) Urquart**

(c) Foskett (d) Shera

14. Which of the following is not associated with communication system?
    (a) Receiver (b) Sender
    (c) Channel **(d) Entropy**
15. One of the following is not an open source software:
    (a) DSpace **(b) Windows**
    (c) Green Stone (d) Linux
16. DESIDOC is documentation centre for:
    (a) Indigenous Knowledge
    (b) Defence Science
    (c) Rural Development
    (d) Khadi & Village Industries
17. Questionnaire is a:
    (a) Research method
    (b) Measurement Technique
    (c) Tool for data collection
    (d) All the above
18. Mean, median and mode are:
    (a) Measures of devotion
    (b) Ways of sampling
    (c) Measures of control tendency
    (d) None of the above
19. 'Cranfield Studies' are an example of:
    (a) Survey Research **(b) Experimental Research**
    (c) Historical Research (d) Case Study
20. **Assertion (A) :** As the level of recall increases, precision tends to decrease.
    Reason (R) : Recall and precision tend to vary inversely

    Codes:
    (a) Both (A) and (R) are true
    (b) (A) is true but (R) is false
    (c) Both are partially true
    (d) (R) is true but (A) is false

21. **Assertion (A) :** Operators using 'AND', 'OR' and 'NOT' are mostly used in online IR.

Reason (R) : User interfaces cannot transform the natural language input into Boolean search query

Codes:

(a) Both (A) and (R) are true

(b) (A) is true but (R) is false

(c) (R) is true but (A) is false

(d) Both (A) and (R) are false

22. **Assertion (A) :** Maximization of the use of documents is the motto of the library.

Reason (R) : Maximization of the use of documents is the motto of the library.

Codes:

(a) Both (A) and (R) are true

(b) Both (A) and (R) are false

(c) (A) is true but (R) is false

(d) (R) is true but (A) is false

23. **Assertion (A):** User profile is an essential component of SDI service.

Reason (R): SDI is a personalized current awareness service.

Codes:

(a) Both (A) and (R) are true

(b) Both (A) and (R) are false

(c) Both are partially true

(d) (A) is true but (R) is false

24. **Assertion (A):** AACR2 like CCC can satisfy all approaches of the users.

Reason (R): Both AACR2 and CCC are comprehensive cataloguing codes.

Codes:

(a) (A) is true and (R) is false

(b) (R) is true but (A) is false

(c) Both (A) and (R) are true

(d) Both (A) and (R) are false

25. **Assertion (A):** Document transfer and information transfer are not the same.

Reason (R): Assimillation of the content of the document by the user constitutes information transfer.

Codes:

(a) (A) is true and (R) is false

(b) (R) is true but (A) is false

(c) Both (A) and (R) are true

(d) Both (A) and (R) are false

26. **Assertion (A):** ISO 9000 is a quality framework which calls for documentation to adopt TQM in a Library.

Reason (R): ISO 9000 is a valuable component of TQM

Codes:

(a) (A) is true and (R) is false

(b) (R) is true but (A) is false

(c) Both (A) and (R) are false

(d) Both (A) and (R) are true

27. **Assertion (A):** Consortia cannot provide an effective strategy to increase the buying power of individual libraries.

Reason (R): Consortia arrangement saves the funds of the libraries in developing their information sources.

(a) (A) is false but (R) is true

(b) (A) is true but (R) is false

(c) Both (A) and (R) are false

(d) Both (A) and (R) are true

28. Arrange the following in the order of computer generations:

(i) Integrated circuit (ii) Transistor

(iii) Vacuum Tube (iv) Chip

Codes:

(a) (iv) (ii) (iii) (i) **(b) (iii) (ii) (iv) (i)**
(c) (i) (ii) (iii) (iv) (d) (iii) (iv) (ii) (i)

Actual order is (iii) (ii) (i) (iv).

29. Match the following:

List-I	**List-II**
(a) BLAISE project	(i) Library of Congress
(b) MARC project	(ii) Intel
(c) Union Catalogue project	(iii) INSDOC
(d) Microchip	(iv) British Library

Codes:

	(a)	(b)	(c)	(d)
(a)	(iii)	(ii)	(iv)	(i)
(b)	**(i)**	**(ii)**	**(iii)**	**(iv)**
(c)	(iv)	(i)	(iii)	(ii)
(d)	(ii)	(iii)	(i)	(iv)

30. Which is the correct logical sequence of the following:
(a) Information, knowledge, data, wisdom
(b) Knowledge, Information, wisdom, data
(c) **Data, knowledge, information, wisdom**
(d) Data, information, knowledge, wisdom

31. Subject indexing systems were developed in the order as:
(a) Chain indexing, Systematic indexing (Kaiser), PRECIS, COMPASS
(b) **Systematic indexing (1911), Chain indexing (1934), PRECIS (1969), COMPASS (1991)**
(c) Systematic indexing, PRECIS, Chain indexing, COMPASS
(d) Systematic indexing, COMPASS, Chain indexing, PRECIS

32. Arrange the following associations in the order of year of establishment:
(a) SIS, IASLIC, IATLIS, ILA
(b) IASLIC, ILA, SIS, IATLIS
(c) ILA, SIS, IASLIC, IATLIS
(d) **ILA (1933), IASLIC (1956), IATLIS (1970), SIS (1976)**

33. Arrange the following Act according to year of enactment:
    (a) Copyright Act, The Patent Act, Information Technology Act, IPR Act
    (b) The Patent Act, Copyright Act, Information Technology Act, IPR Act
    (c) Copyright Act, IPR Act, The Patent Act, Information Technology Act
    (d) **Copyright Act (1957), The Patent Act (1970), IPR Act, Information Technology Act (2006)**
34. Arrange different codes according to year of origin:
    (a) **Anthony Pannizi code (1841), Cutter's rules for dictionary catalogue (1876), classified catalogue code (1934), Anglo American Cataloguing Rules-II (1978)**
    (b) Anthony Pannizi code, classified catalogue code, Cutter's rules for dictionary catalogue, Anglo American Cataloguing Rules-II
    (c) Anthony Pannizi code, Anglo American Cataloguing Rules-II, classified catalogue code, Cutter's rules for dictionary catalogue
    (d) Anthony Pannizi code, Cutter's rules for dictionary catalogue, Anglo American Cataloguing Rules-II, classified catalogue code
35. Arrange the following according to the year of publication:
    (a) Encyclopaedia Britannica, Encyclopedia Americana, Encyclopedia of Library & Information Science, McGraw-Hill Encyclopedia of Science & Technology
    (b) Encyclopaedia Britannica, Encyclopedia of Library & Information Science, McGraw-Hill Encyclopedia of Science & Technology Encyclopedia Americana
    (c) Encyclopaedia Britannica (1768), Encyclopedia Americana (1829), McGraw-Hill Encyclopedia of Science & Technology (1960), Encyclopedia of Library & Information Science (1968)

(d) Encyclopaedia Britannica, McGraw-Hill Encyclopedia of Science & Technology, Encyclopedia Americana, Encyclopedia of Library & Information Science

36. Match the following:

List-I	List-II
(a) Conventional	(i) Patents
(b) Neo-conventional	(ii) Printed Books
(c) Non-conventional	(iii) Satellite imageries
(d) Meta documents	(iv) Audio-visual material

Codes:

	(a)	(b)	(c)	(d)
(a)	(i)	(ii)	(iii)	(iv)
(b)	**(ii)**	**(i)**	**(iv)**	**(iii)**
(c)	(iv)	(i)	(iii)	(ii)
(d)	(iii)	(ii)	(i)	(iv)

37. Match the following:

List-I	List-II
(a) Library is a people's university	(i) Kothari
(b) Library is a growing organisation	(ii) Urquart
(c) Library can be useful to society	(iii) Ranganathan
(d) Library is the heart of the University	(iv) Sayajirao Gayakwad

Codes:

	(a)	(b)	(c)	(d)
(a)	**(iv)**	**(iii)**	**(ii)**	**(i)**
(b)	(iv)	(i)	(iii)	(ii)
(c)	(ii)	(iv)	(iii)	(i)
(d)	(iv)	(ii)	(i)	(iii)

38. Match the following:

List-I	List-II
(a) P.Wassermann	(i) Line of thinking
(b) P.Atherton	(ii) Foundation of Education for Librarianship
(c) J.H.Shera	(iii) New Librarianship
(d) Maurice B.Line	(iv) Putting knowledge to work

Codes:

	(a)	(b)	(c)	(d)
(a)	(i)	(ii)	(iii)	(iv)
(b)	(ii)	(i)	(iii)	(iv)
(c)	**(iv)**	**(iii)**	**(i)**	**(ii)**
(d)	(iii)	(iv)	(ii)	(i)

39. Match the following:

List-I	**List-II**
(a) Theory of X & Y	(i) Frederic Taylor
(b) Scientific Management	(ii) Ouchi
(c) Need hierarchy	(iii) A.Maslow
(d) Theory Z	(iv) D.Mcgregor

Codes:

	(a)	(b)	(c)	(d)
(a)	(iii)	(ii)	(i)	(iv)
(b)	(iv)	(iii)	(ii)	(i)
(c)	(ii)	(i)	(iv)	(iii)
(d)	**(iv)**	**(i)**	**(iii)**	**(ii)**

40. Match the following:

List-I	**List-II**
(a) UDC	(i) H.E.Bliss
(b) DDC	(ii) C.A.Cutter
(c) Expansive classification	(iii) Otlet and La Fontain
(d) Bibliographic classification	(iv) M.Dewey

Codes:

	(a)	(b)	(c)	(d)
(a)	(iii)	(i)	(ii)	(iv)
(b)	**(iii)**	**(iv)**	**(ii)**	**(i)**
(c)	(iii)	(ii)	(iv)	(i)
(d)	(i)	(ii)	(iii)	(iv)

41. Match the following:

List-I	**List-II**
(a) British Library	(i) Russia
(b) Bibliotheque National	(ii) USA
(c) Lenin Library	(iii) UK
(d) Library of Congress	(iv) France

Codes:

	(a)	(b)	(c)	(d)
(a)	(iv)	(iii)	(i)	(ii)
(b)	(i)	(ii)	(iii)	(iv)
(c)	**(iii)**	**(iv)**	**(i)**	**(ii)**
(d)	(iii)	(iv)	(ii)	(i)

42. Matching the following:

List-I	**List-II**
(a) Windows	(i) A revolving disc on which data is stored
(b) Microprocessor	(ii) It is used for processing of text
(c) Wordprocessor	(iii) Collection of programmes for computer system
(d) Software	(iv) A graphical user interface working as DOS

Codes:

	(a)	(b)	(c)	(d)
(a)	**(iv)**	**(i)**	**(ii)**	**(iii)**
(b)	(iii)	(ii)	(i)	(iv)
(c)	(ii)	(iii)	(iv)	(i)
(d)	(i)	(ii)	(iii)	(iv)

43. Match the following:

List-I (Library Act)	**List-II (Year of Enactment)**
(a) Orissa	(i) 2006
(b) Goa	(ii) 2005
(c) Uttaranchal	(iii) 2001
(d) Uttar Pradesh	(iv) 1994

Codes:

	(a)	(b)	(c)	(d)
(a)	(i)	(ii)	(iii)	(iv)
(b)	**(iii)**	**(iv)**	**(ii)**	**(i)**
(c)	(iv)	(iii)	(ii)	(i)
(d)	(ii)	(i)	(iii)	(iv)

44. Match the following:

List-I	**List-II**
(a) Software	(i) Key board
(b) Hardware	(ii) CD
(c) Storage Device	(iii) SOUL
(d) I/O Device	(iv) CPU

Codes:

	(a)	(b)	(c)	(d)
(a)	(ii)	(iv)	(iii)	(i)
(b)	(ii)	(iii)	(iv)	(i)
(c)	(iii)	(ii)	(iv)	(i)
(d)	**(iii)**	**(iv)**	**(ii)**	**(i)**

45. Match the following:

List-I	**List-II**
(a) Planning	(i) Delegation of authority
(b) Staffing	(ii) Audit
(c) Control	(iii) Promotion
(d) Organising	(iv) Resource management

Codes:

	(a)	(b)	(c)	(d)
(a)	(i)	(ii)	(iii)	(iv)
(b)	(ii)	(iv)	(i)	(iii)
(c)	(iii)	(i)	(ii)	(iv)
(d)	**(iv)**	**(iii)**	**(ii)**	**(i)**

COMPREHENSION TEST:

46. Which factors force organisation to use IT to harness information?
    (a) Explosion of sources of information
    (b) Availability of latest information on real time basis
    (c) Time, volume and complex nature of information on real time basis
    (d) Information needs of users are inter-disciplinary in nature

47. Major obstacle in taking accurate futuristic decisions is;
    (a) availability of more information
    (b) cut-throat competition
    (c) Everchanging socio-economic and political situations
    (d) Globalisation
48. Which is the most appropriate tool to make better use of information?
    (a) Well qualified and experienced information professional
    (b) Depth classification and indexing
    (c) Experts in domain knowledge
    (d) Information technology
49. What is the critical characteristic of information delivery system for making its use effective?
    (a) Efficient channels of communication system
    (b) Ability to develop appropriate information products
    (c) Right information, delivered at right time
    (d) Developing quality photocopying and fax facility
50. What is the crucial decision for an organisation to take to beat the competition?
    (a) To create a mechanism to access, organise and process information within an organisation
    (b) To establish a separate department for acquiring and processing information
    (c) To strengthen the libraries already existing in the organisation
    (d) To collaborate with university and national and international information systems.

December 2008

1. Who is the Chairman of National Knowledge Commission?
   (a) Harsha Parekh (b) P.B.Mangla
   (c) Kalpana Dasgupta **(d) Sam Pitroda**
2. Which is the primary source for finding out Indian periodicals in Agriculture?
   (a) Ulrich International Periodical Directory
   (b) Reference Asia
   (c) Press in India
   (d) INFA Yearbook
3. Which of the following indexes only papers presented in the conferences?
   (a) LISA
   (b) Current Research Abstracts
   (c) Reseach-in-Progress
   (d) ISTP
4. IATLIS is an association of:
   (a) Library Science Faculty
   (b) Special Librarians
   (c) Librarians of Public Libraries
   (d) Librarians of Teachers' Training Colleges
5. Appropriate communication media for CD-Net is
   (a) Twisted wires **(b) Optical fibre**
   (c) Co-axial cables (d) Ethernet cables
6. Identify the association that has changed its original name
   (a) ILA (b) SLA
   (c) LA (d) ALA
7. Recall and Precision ratios are used in the evaluation of
   (a) Reference service
   (b) Information retrieval
   (c) Bibliographic service
   (d) Document delivery service

8. Number of digits in ISBN now are
   (a) 10 digits (b) 11 digits
   (c) 12 digits **(d) 13 digits**
9. 'Emerald' is the database of
   (a) Gems and jewelary literature
   (b) Medical Science literature
   (c) Library and Information Science literature
   (d) Earth Science literature
10. TQM was promulgated by
    (a) Deming and Juran (b) Maslow
    (c) Drucker (d) Taylor
11. MESH is the name of
    (a) Medical Library **(b) Controlled Vocabulary**
    (c) Online database (d) CSIR Unit
12. 'Rules for dictionary catalogue' was devised by
    (a) A.Panizzi (b) C.C.Jewet
    (c) S.Lubetzky **(d) C.A.Cutter**
13. A gazette gives information about
    (a) Places of tourist interest
    (b) History of places
    (c) Official announcement and notification
    (d) Old records
14. Glossary is a
    (a) List of technical words with definitions
    (b) List of words in a language
    (c) List of thematically arranged words
    (d) Alphabetical index to passages of work
15. National Library for Blind and handicapped of India is located
    (a) Madras (b) Tanjore
    (c) Dehradun (d) Delhi
16. The term 'Information Retrieval' was coined by
    (a) H.P.Luhn **(b) Calvin Mooers**
    (c) Mortimer Taube (d) Derek Austin

17. The term 'hypertext' was coined by

    (a) Vannever Bush (b) John Brown

    (c) M.C.Kith **(d) Ted Nelson**

18. With which agency did UNESCO collaborate to establish UNISIST?

    (a) **ICSU** (b) FID

    (c) IFLA (d) ILA

19. Which university appointed the first full time university librarian?

    (a) Delhi University (b) Punjab University

    (c) Madras University (d) Calcutta University

20. **Assertion (A) :** Classification and indexing have always been of central intellectual interest in IR

    Reason (R) : Conceptual analysis of the content of the queries and documents are essential input to an IR system.

    Code:

    (a) (A) is true and (R) is false

    (b) (R) is true and (A) is false

    (c) Both (A) and (R) are true

    (d) (A) and (R) both are partially true

21. **Assertion (A):** Any change in the environment of the subject can not affect the state of the subject

    Reason (R): A subject can be viewed as a system consisting of a set of interacting component ideas.

    Code:

    (a) (A) is true and (R) is false

    (b) (R) is true and (A) is false

    (c) Both (A) and (R) are true

    (d) Both (A) and (R) are false

22. **Assertion (A):** Action research is a form of interpretive research to study human actions and social practices for immediate application.

Reason (R): Action research is an applied research, which is focussed on the solution to local problems, not to develop any theory for general application.

Code:

(a) (A) is true and (R) is false

(b) (R) is true and (A) is false

(c) Both (A) and (R) are false

(d) Both (A) and (R) are true

23. **Assertion (A):** Information systems support promotion of research, development and innovation relating to the national development of a country.

Reason (R): Information is the basic input to the development.

Code:

(a) Both (A) and (R) are true and (R) is not the correct explanation

(b) Both (A) and (R) is the correct explanation

(c) (A) is true but (R) is false

(d) (A) is false but (R) is true

24. **Assertion (A):** Many projects and initiatives are taken to create digital libraries.

Reason (R): Digital library improves the professional status of librarians.

Code:

(a) Both (A) and (R) are true

(b) Both (A) and (R) are false

(c) (A) is true but (R) is the correct explanation

(d) (A) is false but (R) is true

25. **Assertion (a) :** IFLA's UBC programme encourages the use and exchange of standardised bibliographic description.

Reason (R) : Use of standard enables to bring uniformity in bibliographic description and interchange of bibliographic data.

Code:

(a) Both (A) and (R) are false

(b) Both (A) and (R) are true

(c) (R) is true but (A) is false

(d) (A) is true but (R) is false

26. **Assertion (A) :** UNESCO championed the cause of public library movement.

Reason (R) : UNESCO's concern for public library movement is reflected in its 'Public Library Manifesto'.

Code:

(a) (A) is true but (R) is false

(b) (A) is false but (R) is true

(c) Both (A) and (R) are false

(d) Both (A) and (R) are true

27. **Assertion (A) :** PRECIS is not based upon any particular system of classification.

Reason (R) : PRECIS is not built around any theoretical ideas on classification.

Code:

(a) (A) is true but (R) is false

(b) (A) is false but (R) is true

(c) Both (A) and (R) are true

(d) Both (A) and (R) are true

28. Arrange according to year of establishment.

(a) Chemical Abstracts (1907), Biological Abstracts (1926), Science Citation index (1961), Indian Science Abstracts (1965)

(b) Chemical Abstracts, Science Citation Index, Indian Science Index, Indian Science Abstracts

(c) Biological Abstracts, Chemical Abstracts, Science Citation Index, Indian Science Abstracts

(d) Chemical Abstracts, Biological Abstracts, Indian Science Abstracts, Science Citation Index

29. The correct sequence of information flow is:

(a) Message Source Channel Receiver

(b) **Source Message Channel Receiver**
(c) Message Channel Source Receiver
(d) Message Channel Receiver Source

30. Arrange the following classification schemes in the order of year of origin
(a) UDC, Expansive classification, DDC, CC
(b) Expansive classification, UDC, CC, DDC
(c) DDC, CC, Expansive classification, UDC
(d) **DDC, Expansive classification, UDC, CC**

31. Arrange the following Public Library Acts according to the year of enactment
(a) Manipur Public Libraries Act, West Bengal Public Libraries Act, Kerala Public Libraries Act, Mizoram Public Libraries Act
(b) West Bengal Public Libraries Act (1979), Manipur Public Libraries Act (1988), Kerala Public Libraries Act (1989), Mizoram Public Libraries Act (1993)
(c) West Bengal Public Libraries Act, Kerala Public Libraries Act, Manipur Public Libraries Act, Mizoram Public Libraries Act
(d) West Bengal Public Libraries Act, Manipur Public Libraries Act, Mizoram Public Libraries Act, Kerala Public Libraries Act

32. Arrange the following Assiciations according to the year of establishment
(a) ALA (1876), CILIP (LA) (1877), Special Library Association (1908), ASLIB (1924)
(b) CILIP (LA), ALA, Special Library Asslociation, ASLIB
(c) ALA, Special Library Association, CILIP (LA), ASLIB
(d) ASLIB, ALA, CILIP (LA), Special Library Association

33. Arrange the following Standards according to the year of their introduction.
(a) ISBN, ICCP, CCF, ISDS
(b) CCF, ICCP, ISBN, ISDS
(c) ICCP(1961), ISBN (1970), ISDS, CCF (1978)
(d) ISDS, ISBN, ICCP, CCF

34. Match the following items given in List – I and List – II

List-I	List-II
(a) Principles of librarianship	(i) Berwick Sayers
(b) Practical guidelines for classification	(ii) S.R.Ranganathan
(c) Rules for Dictionary cataloguing	(iii) D.J.Urquart
(d) Five Laws of library science	(iv) C.A.Cutter

Codes:

	(a)	(b)	(c)	(d)
(a)	**(iii)**	**(i)**	**(iv)**	**(ii)**
(b)	(i)	(ii)	(iii)	(iv)
(c)	(iii)	(ii)	(iv)	(i)
(d)	(i)	(iii)	(iv)	(ii)

35. Match the following items given in List – I and List – II

List-I	List-II
(a) Informatique	(i) English
(b) Informatik	(ii) Italian
(c) Informatica	(iii) French
(d) Informatics	(iv) German

Codes:

	(a)	(b)	(c)	(d)
(a)	**(iii)**	**(iv)**	**(ii)**	**(i)**
(b)	(ii)	(i)	(iv)	(iii)
(c)	(iv)	(iii)	(i)	(II)
(d)	(iii)	(i)	(ii)	(iv)

36. Match the following items given in List – I and List – II

List-I	List-II
(a) Bibliographic description	(i) Current Awareness Service
(b) Short-range reference service	(ii) Post Coordinating Indexing
(c) SDI	(iii) Abstract
(d) Uniterm	(iv) Ready Reference Source

Codes:

	(a)	(b)	(c)	(d)
(a)	(iii)	(iv)	(i)	(ii)
(b)	(ii)	(i)	(iii)	(iv)
(c)	(iv)	(i)	(ii)	(iii)
(d)	(ii)	(iii)	(iv)	(i)

37. Arrange the following according to their increasing storage capacity.

(i) Catridge (ii) CD-ROM

(iii) Floppy disks (iv) DVD

Codes:

	(a)	(b)	(c)	(d)
(a)	**(iii)**	**(i)**	**(ii)**	**(iv)**
(b)	(i)	(ii)	(iii)	(iv)
(c)	(iv)	(iii)	(i)	(ii)
(d)	(i)	(iii)	(ii)	(iv)

38. Match the following items given in List – I and List – II

List-I	**List-II**
(a) DDC 19th edition	(i) John Camaroni
(b) DDC 20th edition	(ii) Melvil Dewey
(c) DDC 21st edition	(iii) John Mitchell
(d) DDC 22nd edition	(iv) Benjamin Custer

Codes:

	(a)	(b)	(c)	(d)
(a)	(ii)	(iv)	(iii)	(i)
(b)	**(ii)**	**(i)**	**(iv)**	**(iii)**
(c)	(ii)	(iv)	(i)	(iii)
(d)	(iv)	(iii)	(ii)	(i)

39. Match the following items given in List – I and List – II

List-I	**List-II**
(a) Nascent micro thought	(i) Colon classification
(b) Acess points	(ii) Motivation
(c) Physiological needs	(iii) Documentation
(d) Analytico –synthetic classification	(iv) AACR II

Codes:

	(a)	(b)	(c)	(d)
(a)	(iii)	(iv)	(ii)	(i)
(b)	**(iii)**	**(ii)**	**(i)**	**(iv)**
(c)	(ii)	(i)	(iv)	(iii)
(d)	(i)	(ii)	(iii)	(iv)

40. Match the following:

List-I	**List-II**
(a) SHE	(i) Nuclear Energy
(b) MESH	(ii) Education
(c) ERIC	(iii) Medicine
(d) INIS	(iv) Engineering

Codes:

	(a)	(b)	(c)	(d)
(a)	(i)	(iii)	(ii)	(iv)
(b)	**(iv)**	**(iii)**	**(ii)**	**(i)**
(c)	(ii)	(iii)	(i)	(iv)
(d)	(i)	(ii)	(iii)	(iv)

41. Match the following:

List-I	**List-II**
(a) Five Laws of Library Science	(i) C.D.Needham
(b) Subject approach to information	(ii) R.Ranganathan
(c) Organising Knowledge in Libraries	(iii) B.C.Vickery and A.Vickery
(d) Information Science in theory and practice	(v) A.C.Foskett

Codes:

	(a)	(b)	(c)	(d)
(a)	**(ii)**	**(iv)**	**(i)**	**(iii)**
(b)	(i)	(iii)	(iv)	(ii)
(c)	(iii)	(ii)	(iv)	(i)
(d)	(iv)	(ii)	(iii)	(i)

42. Match the following:

List-I	**List-II**
(a) Melvil Dewey	(i) Belgium
(b) Berwick Sayers	(ii) USA
(c) B.S.Kesavan	(iii) Britain
(d) Paul Otlet	(v) India

Codes:

	(a)	(b)	(c)	(d)
(a)	(ii)	(iv)	(i)	(iii)
(b)	(iv)	(iii)	(i)	(ii)
(c)	**(ii)**	**(iii)**	**(iv)**	**(i)**
(d)	(ii)	(i)	(iii)	(iv)

43. Match the following:

List-I	**List-II**
(a) UBC	(i) FID
(b) UDC	(ii) IFLA
(c) MARC	(iii) ASTINFO
(d) Document Supply System	(v) Library of Congress

Codes:

	(a)	(b)	(c)	(d)
(a)	(ii)	(iv)	(i)	(iii)
(b)	**(ii)**	**(i)**	**(iv)**	**(iii)**
(c)	(i)	(ii)	(iii)	(iv)
(d)	(iii)	(ii)	(iv)	(i)

44. Match the following:

List-I	**List-II**
(a) Bradford's law	(i) Author's production
(b) MESH	(ii) Citation indexing
(c) ERIC	(iii) Word frequency
(d) INIS	(v) Scattering

Codes:

	(a)	(b)	(c)	(d)
(a)	(i)	(ii)	(iv)	(iii)
(b)	(iii)	(iv)	(ii)	(i)
(c)	(iv)	(ii)	(i)	(iii)
(d)	**(iv)**	**(i)**	**(ii)**	**(iii)**

45. Match the following:

List-I	List-II
(a) Mission Oriented	(i) Patent Information System
(b) Social Science Oriented	(ii) DESIDOC
(c) ERIC	(iii) NISSAT
(d) INIS	(v) NASSDOC

Codes:

	(a)	(b)	(c)	(d)
(a)	**(iii)**	**(iv)**	**(ii)**	**(i)**
(b)	(iv)	(iii)	(ii)	(i)
(c)	(i)	(ii)	(iii)	(iv)
(d)	(ii)	(iii)	(iv)	(i)

COMPREHENSION TEST:

46. The following system can survive in isolation:
    (a) Accounting system
    (b) Planning system
    (c) Inventory management system
    (d) No system
47. If anyone wants information from two systems, he must get the information:
    (a) From each system and correlate
    (b) from one system at a time for correlation
    (c) from two systems and need not correlate
    (d) from as many systems as possible and correlate
48. All the systems must be integrated for:
    (a) Isolation (b) proper planning
    (c) dramatic impact (d) hhuge profit
49. Collecting and arranging data is:
    (a) Needed for library personnel
    (b) needed for the functioning department
    (c) needed for production planning
    (d) needed for purchase department only
50. The executives and managers cannot make good decisions:

(a) With the isolated data
(b) only when they collate the data them-self
(c) only when they were produced with the required information
(d) when they have lost valuable time

December 2009

1. The quotation "Where is the Wisdom, We Lost in Knowledge.." is by
(a) John Keats (b) M.P.Carter
(c) T.S.Eliot (d) Marshall McLuhan

2. Entropy is a measure of
(a) Degree of relevance of information
(b) Quantity of irrelevant information
(c) Degree of uncertainty in information
(d) Degree of certainty in information

3. CONPOLIS (India) was set up in the year
(a) 1985 (b) 1986
(c) 1987 (d) 1988

4. First time efforts for the development of libraries in India were made
(a) S.R.Ranganathan (b) S.Radhakrishnan
(c) Sayaji Rao Gaekwad I **(d) Sayaji Rao Gaekwad II**

5. An E-book which does not require an internet connection to access its contents is
(a) Web book (b) Palm book
(c) Electronic Ink e-book **(d) Digital book**

6. Emerald full text database is published from
(a) USA (b) Germany
(c) France (d) UK

7. Who propounded 'Conservative, moderate and liberal theories of reference service'?
(a) William A.Katz (b) S.R.Ranganathan
(c) James I. Wyer (d) R.Emery

8. The input centre for INIS in India is

(a) DRDO (b) DSIR
(c) TFIR **(d) BARC**

9. The provision of phase relations in DDC was made available from
   (a) 14th edition (b) 2nd edition
   (c) 7th edition (d) 11th edition
10. RDA stands for
    (a) Resource Description Agency
    (b) Reference Description and Access
    (c) Reference Description Agency
    (d) Resource Description and Access
11. Cost benefit analysis means
    (a) Value for money
    (b) Performance evaluation based on cost
    (c) Finding out unit cost
    (d) Performance evaluation based on inputs
12. Which national agency in India is assigning the ISBN?
    (a) Raja Ram Mohan Roy National Education Resource Centre
    (b) Delhi Public Library
    (c) Federation of Publishers in India
    (d) National Library of India
13. The term 'Cyberspace' was first used by
    (a) Andrew Pollock **(b) William Gibson**
    (c) John Postal (d) Joe Flower
14. RFID Technology is used in
    (a) Acquisition (b) Serial Control
    (c) Circulation Control (d) OPAC
15. The Boolean operator 'AND' is related to
    (a) Productive **(b) Additive**
    (c) Logical Difference (d) None of the above
16. The process of configuring the disks into tracks and sectors is called
    (a) Booting (b) Formatting
    (c) Labelling (d) All the above

17. A research design is
    (a) A series of guide posts
    (b) A series of sampling
    (c) A hypothetical statement
    (d) A controller of variance
18. In a questionnaire, questionnaire on age, income and gender are the examples of
    (a) Dependent variable (b) Intervening variables
    (c) Independent variables (d) Manipulation variables
19. The simple Dublin Core Metadata Element Set (DCMES) consists of
    (a) 10 elements **(b) 15 elements**
    (c) 14 elements (d) 18 elements
20. 'Libraries as Gateways to Knowledge' is the title of the document
    (a) National Information Policy, 1986
    (b) Information Technology Act, 2000
    (c) National Knowledge Commission on Libraries, 2007
    (d) None of the above
21. **Assertion (A):** INDEST conceived J-Gate as a customized gate for e-journals subscribed by the member libraries
    Reason (R): J-Gate provides a common access platform for all its members to search and share resources subscribed by the member libraries.
    Codes:
    (a) Both (A) and (R) are true and (R) is the correct explanation
    (b) Both (A) and (R) are true but (R) is not the correct explanation
    (c) (A) is true but (R) is false
    (d) (A) is false but (R) is true
22. **Assertion (A):** XML, just like HTML is a meta language that is capable of containing extendable elements.

Reason (R): XML develop and deploy new specific mark up, enabling automatic authoring and processing of networked information.

Codes:

(a) Is false but (R) is true.

(b) Both (A) and (R) are true and (R) is not the correct explanation.

(c) (A) is true and (R) is false

(d) Both (A) and (R) are true.

23. **Assertion (A):** Measuring the Internet and in particular the web is a difficult task.

Reason (R): Web is considered as a new publishing medium with inadequate editorial process.

Codes:

(a) Both (A) and (R) are true and (R) is the correct explanation.

(b) Both (A) and (R) are true and (R) is not the correct explanation

(c) (A) is true but (R) is false

(d) (A) is false but (R) is true

24. **Assertion (A):** Ann indexing language is an artificial language as it uses controlled vocabulary.

Reason (R): It provides different relationships between terms.

Codes:

(a) Both (A) and (R) are false

(b) Both (A) and (R) are true.

(c) (A) is true but (R) is false.

(d) (A) is false but (R) is true.

25. **Assertion (A):** With large collection of documents, recall can be measured properly.

Reason(R): The proper estimation of maximum recall for a query requires detailed knowledge of all the documents in the collection.

Codes:

(a) Both (A) and (R) are true

(b) Both (A) and (R) are true and (R) is not the correct explanation.

(c) (A) is true but (R) is false

(d) (A) is false but (R) is true

26. **Assertion (A):** In contemporary digital environment, IPR become the focal point.

Reason (R): Many fold increase of unfair use of I.P.

Codes:

(a) (A) and (R) are true

(b) (A) and (R) are false.

(c) (A) is true and (R) is false

(d) (A) is false and (R) is true.

27. **Assertion (A):** Library automation is at a slow pace in Indian Libraries.

Reason (R): Lack of UGC (India) support lead to this situation.

Codes:

(a) Both (A) and (R) are true

(b) Both (A) and (R) are false.

(c) (A) is true but (R) is false

(d) (A) is false but (R) is true.

28. **Assertion (A):** The development of Institutional Repositories in India is at a slow pace.

Reason (R): This can be attributed to the non-availability of open source software and lack of interest among the LIS professionals.

Codes:

(a) Both (A) and (R) are true

(b) Both (A) and (R) are false.

(c) (A) is true but (R) is partially true

(d) (A) is false and (R) is true

29. **Assertion (A):** Subject gateways offer the users an alternative to 'vacuum Cleaner' type of search engines, such as Google, Infoseek, Alta Vista etc.

    Reason (R): Subject gateways hold manually created records, rich resource description containing relevant information.

    Codes:

    (a) Both (A) and (R) are true.

    (b) Both (A) and (R) are true and (R) is not the correct explanation

    (c) (A) is true but (R) is false

    (d) (A) is false but (R) is true

30. **Assertion (A):** Para-professional staff support the professional staff in Library routines.

    Reason (R): Para-professional staff acquire skill by experience

    Codes:

    (a) (A) is false but (R) is true

    (b) (A) is true but (R) is false

    (c) Both (A) and (R) are false

    (d) Both (A) and (R) are true

31. Public Library Law has already been passed in the following States. Identify the correct chronological order in which they were enacted.

    Codes:

    (i) Uttaranchal (Uttarakhand)

    (ii) Orissa

    (iii) Gujarat

    (iv) Haryana

    (a) (i), (ii), (iii), (iv) (b) (iv), (ii), (i), (iii)

    (c) (ii), (iii), (iv), (i) (d) (iii), (ii), (i), (iv)

32. Arrange in chronological order the following persons who were associated with computing history:

    (i) J.Presper Eckart (ii) John W. Mauchly

    (iii) August Ada (iv) Charles Babbage

Codes:

(a) (iii) (ii) (i) (iv) (b) (ii) (i) (iii) (iv)

(c) (i) (iv) (iii) (ii) (d) **(iv) (iii) (ii) (i)**

33. Arrange the following events of Public Library movement in chronological order:

(i) Enact of Press and Registration of Books Act (1867)

(ii) Establishment of the Punjab Library, Lahore

(iii) Constitution of Fyzee Committee

(iv) Declaration of Imperial Library (Calcutta) as National Library of India (1948)

Codes:

(a) **(i) (iii) (iv) (ii)** (b) (i) (ii) (iii) (iv)

(c) (ii) (iii) (iv) (i) (d) (iv) (i) (iii) (ii)

34. Arrange the following layers of OSI model in the sequence in which they function:

(i) Network Layer (ii) Physical Layer

(iii) Transport Layer (iv) Data Link Layer

Codes:

(a) (iii) (iv) (ii) (i) (b) (iv) (ii) (i) (iii)

(c) (ii) (iv) (i) (iii) (d) (i) (ii) (iii) (iv)

35. Arrange the following four quadrants of spiral of scientific method in their logical order:

(i) Ascendant (ii) Nadir

(iii) Zenith (iv) Descendent

Codes:

(a) (iv) (i) (iii) (ii) (b) (i) (iii) (iv) (ii)

(c) (iii) (ii) (i) (iv) **(d) (ii) (i) (iii) (iv)**

36. Arrange the following books in order of their publication:

(i) Classified Catalogue Code (1934)

(ii) Prolegomena to Library Classification (1937)

(iii) Five Laws of Library Science (1931)

(iv) Colon Classification (1933)

Codes:

(a) (i) (iv) (iii) (ii) (b) (iii) (ii) (iv) (i)

(c) (iii) (iv) (i) (ii) (d) (iv) (i) (ii) (iii)

37. Arrange the following bibliographies according to their date of origin:

(i) Indian National Bibliography

(ii) Cumulative Book Index

(iii) Book in Print

(iv) British National Bibliography

Codes:

(a) (iii) (iv) (i) (ii) (b) (ii) (iii) (iv) (i)

(c) (i) (ii) (iii) (iv) (d) (iv) (ii) (i) (iii)

38. Arrange the following schemes of classification according to their year of origin:

(i) Colon Classification

(ii) Expansive Classification

(iii) Universal Decimal Classification

(iv) Dewey Decimal Classification

Codes:

(a) (ii) (iii) (iv) (i) (b) (iii) (iv) (i) (ii)

(c) (iv) (ii) (iii) (i) (d) (i) (ii) (iv) (iii)

39. Arrange the following principles and canon according to their levels as enunciated by Dr. S.R.Ranganathan

(i) Principles of Cataloguing

(ii) General Normative Principles

(iii) Laws of Library Science

(iv) Canons of Cataloguing

Codes:

	(a)	(b)	(c)	(d)
(a)	(i)	(iv)	(iii)	(ii)
(b)	**(ii)**	**(iii)**	**(iv)**	**(i)**
(c)	(ii)	(i)	(iv)	(iii)
(d)	(i)	(iv)	(ii)	(iii)

40. Arrange the following Associations according to their year of formation:

(i) ASLIB (ii) LA

(iii) ALA (iv) SLA

Codes:

	(a)	(b)	(c)	(d)
(a)	**(iii)**	**(ii)**	**(iv)**	**(i)**
(b)	(ii)	(iv)	(i)	(iii)
(c)	(iii)	(i)	(iv)	(ii)
(d)	(iv)	(i)	(iii)	(ii)

41. Match the following:

List-I	**List-II**
(a) Little Science, Big Science	(i) S.C.Bradford
(b) Documentation	(ii) William Martin
(c) The third Wave	(iii) Eric J de Solla Price
(d) The Information Society	(iv) Alwin Toffler

Codes:

	(a)	(b)	(c)	(d)
(a)	(i)	(ii)	(iii)	(iv)
(b)	**(iii)**	**(i)**	**(iv)**	**(ii)**
(c)	(iv)	(iii)	(ii)	(i)
(d)	(ii)	(i)	(iv)	(iii)

42. Match the following:

List-I	**List-II**
(a) Key Word Indexing	(i) J.R.Sharp
(b) Citation Indexing	(ii) H.P.Luhn
(c) Uniterm Indexing	(iii) E.Garfield
(d) SLIC Indexing	(iv) M.Taube

Codes:

	(a)	(b)	(c)	(d)
(a)	**(ii)**	**(iii)**	**(iv)**	**(i)**
(b)	(iii)	(iv)	(i)	(ii)
(c)	(iv)	(i)	(iii)	(ii)
(d)	(i)	(iii)	(ii)	(iv)

43. Match the following:

List-I	**List-II**
(a) Web Navigation Element	(i) Telecommunication
(b) Shift+Tab	(ii) SQL
(c) ANSI Standard	(iii) Hyperlink
(d) TELNET	(iv) Select the previous link

Codes:

	(a)	(b)	(c)	(d)
(a)	(i)	(ii)	(iii)	(iv)
(b)	(iv)	(iii)	(ii)	(i)
(c)	**(iii)**	**(iv)**	**(ii)**	**(i)**
(d)	(ii)	(iii)	(i)	(iv)

44. Match the following:

List-I	**List-II**
(a) Macfee	(i) DOAJ
(b) Directory	(ii) Antivirus
(c) Personal Web pages	(iii) Vendor on Internet
(d) Amazon.com	(iv) Blogs

Codes:

	(a)	(b)	(c)	(d)
(a)	**(ii)**	**(i)**	**(iv)**	**(iii)**
(b)	(i)	(iv)	(iii)	(ii)
(c)	(ii)	(iii)	(iv)	(i)
(d)	(iv)	(iii)	(ii)	(i)

45. Match the following:

List-I	**List-II**
(a) Theory of Knowledge	(i) Farmington Plan
(b) IS: 1553-1960	(ii) Metadata Format
(c) Resource Sharing	(iii) Library Building
(d) TEI	(iv) Epistomology

Codes:

	(a)	(b)	(c)	(d)
(a)	(i)	(iii)	(ii)	(iv)
(b)	(ii)	(iii)	(i)	(iv)
(c)	**(iv)**	**(iii)**	**(i)**	**(ii)**
(d)	(iii)	(i)	(ii)	(iv)

COMPREHENSION TEST:

46. Rolland Munro described accountability as
    (a) Classified documentary artifacts
    (b) Formal artifacts only
    (c) Unpublished and published documents
    (d) Informal, formal and documentary records

47. The phrase 'record keeping' is associated with
    (a) Computer programmers
    (b) Archivists
    (c) Chartered Accounts
    (d) Office Managers
48. What integral components Munro has identified for accounting in the business?
    (a) Records and Codes (b) Documentary archives
    (c) Materials and devices (d) Legal Regulations
49. In general usage accountability means
    (a) Something done informally
    (b) Something achieved
    (c) Something done continuously
    (d) All of the above
50. Accountability, which is represented by an artefact, includes
    (a) Process, Records, People
    (b) Theory, Practice, Records
    (c) Theory, Practice, People
    (d) People, Records, Accounts

June 2010

1. Who expressed knowledge in a simple mathematical equation k(s)+?1=k(s+?s)?
   (a) Fritz Machlup **(b) B.C.Brooks**
   (c) N.J.Belkin (d) C.E.Shannon
2. Which is not a near synonym term to information?
   (a) Ideas (b) Data
   (c) Catalogue (d) Facts
3. CCF stands for
   (a) Common Communication Format
   (b) Centre for Communication Format
   (c) Committee for Communication Format
   (d) Common Curriculum Format

4. Resources sharing among libraries was prompted by the factors
   (a) Price escalation (b) Information explosion
   (c) Both (a) and B) (d) None of the above
5. The Library Association (UK) is now the component of
   (a) ASLIB **(b) CILIP**
   (c) ALA (d) None of the above
6. Which of the following professional Associations does not exist now?
   (a) IFLA **(b) FID**
   (c) ALA (d) IALSIC
7. Real Time Access refers to
   (a) Access in advance
   (b) Access after some time
   (c) Access when searched for
   (d) None of the above
8. Theory X and Theory Y relate to
   (a) Planning **(b) Motivation**
   (c) Innovation (d) None of the above
9. Dewey Decimal Classification is now looked after by
   (a) Lake Placid Club (b) Library of Congress
   (c) OCLC (d) Classification Research Group
10. INSDOC has been merged with NISCOM and is now known as
    (a) DELNET **(b) NISCAIR**
    (c) DESIDOC (d) NASSDOC
11. World Wide Web was first designed by
    (a) Charles Babbage (b) F.W.Lancaster
    (c) Ted Nelson **(d) Tim Berner's Lee**
12. ISBN consists of
    (a) 6 digits (b) 8 digits
    (c) 13 digits (d) 15 digits
13. Bibliographic coupling is needed to
    (a) Bibliometric studies
    (b) Bibliography compilation

(c) Modes of subject formation
(d) Vocabulary control

14. Dublin core meta data consists of
(a) 15 elements (b) 10 elements
(c) 25 elements (d) 08 elements

15. A type of indexing where terms are coordinated prior to searching
(a) Post coordinate indexing
(b) Pre coordinate indexing
(c) Uniterm indexing
(d) None of the above

16. Use of integrated circuits was made in
(a) First Generation Computers
(b) Secord Generation Computers
(c) Third Generation Computers
(d) Fourth Generation Computers

17. The Network Topology in which nodes are connected to a central hub is known as
(a) Ring Topology (b) Bus Topology
(c) Star Topology (d) Mesh Topology

18. Which of the following is a term used for working assumption of a solution to a problem?
(a) Research **(b) Hypothesis**
(c) Bibliography (d) Thesis

19. Computer Memory is measured in
(a) Bytes (b) Kilobytes
(c) Megabytes **(d) All of the above**

20. DELNET stands for
(a) Developing Library Network
(b) Department of Electronics Library Network
(c) Distance Education Library Network
(d) Delhi Library Network

21. **Assertion (A):** Demand is the only governing factor in Book selection.
Reason (R): Patrons' requirements govern building library collections.

Codes:

(a) (A) is true and (R) is false

(b) (A) is false and (R) is true

(c) (A) and (R) both are true

(d) (A) and (R) both are false

22. **Assertion (A):** An indexing language is much more than a list of index terms that are acceptable to users.

Reason (R): An indexing language helps users discriminate between terms and reduces ambiguity in the language.

Codes:

(a) Both (A) and (R) are true and (R) is not the correct explanation.

(b) Both (A) and (R) are true and (R) is the correct explanation.

(c) (A) is false but (R) is true

(d) (A) is true but (R) is false

23. **Assertion (A):** Libraries are facing a threat and are bound to disappear soon.

Reason (R): Internet and WWW provide access to Oceans of information Worldwide.

Codes:

(a) (A) is true but (R) is false

(b) (A) is false but (R) is true

(c) Both (A) and (R) is true

(d) Both (a) and (R) is false

24. **Assertion (A):** Deacidification is a measure to preserve documents in any medium.

Reason (R): Digital preservation needs a different preservation care.

Codes:

(a) (A) is false, but (R) is true

(b) (A) is true but (R) is false

(c) Both (A) and (R) are true

(d) Both (A) and (R) are false

25. **Assertion (A):** SDI is a user oriented current information service.

Reason (R): It is an alerting service directed towards groups.

Codes:

(a) Both (A) and (R) are true

(b) (A) is true, but (R) is false

(c) (A) is false but (R) is true

(d) Both (A) and (R) are false

26. **Assertion (A):** Indexing periodical retrieves information, which includes brief summary of the article.

Reason (R): It provides list of articles alongwith the title, authors and other bibliographic details.

Codes:

(a) Both (A) and (R) are true

(b) Both (A) and (R) are false

(c) (A) is true, but (R) is false

(d) (A) is false but (R) are true

27. **Assertion (A):** Median is simply the middle value when the data have been arranged in ascending or descending order.

Reason (R) : Median refers to the middle value in a distribution

Codes:

(a) Both (A) and (R) are true

(b) (A) is true but (R) is false

(c) (A) is false but (R) is true

(d) Both (A) and (R) are false

28. **Assertion (A):** Database is a collection of interrelated data stored together

Reason (R): It is an organised, integrated collection of data

Codes:

(a) Both (A) and (R) are false

(b) (A) is false but (R) is true

(c) Both (A) and (R) are true

(d) (a) is true but (R) is false

29. **Assertion (A):** Dewey Decimal is an enumerative scheme of classification

Reason (R): The scheme has developed several devices and is no more an enumerative scheme of classification

Codes:

(a) (A) is true but (R) is false

(b) (A) is not true but (R) is true

(c) Both (A) and (R) are true

(d) Both (a) and (R) are false

30. **Assertion (A):** A Library legislation provides proper governance and management

Reason (R): It ensures free public library service to all irrespective of caste, creed and sex

Codes:

(a) Both (A) and (R) are true

(b) Both (A) and (R) are false

(c) (A) is true but (R) is false

(d) (A) is false but (R) is true

31. Arrange the following in the chronological sequence of their development

(i) ISBD (ii) CCF

(iii) FRBR (iv) MARC

Codes:

(a) (i), (ii), (iv), (iii) **(b) (iv), (i), (ii), (iii)**

(c) (iii), (ii), (iv), (i) (d) (i), (iv), (ii), (iii)

32. Arrange the following secondary publications according to the beginning of their publication in chronological order

(i) Biological Abstracts (1926)

(ii) Chemical Abstracts (1907)

(iii) LISA

(iv) Index Medicus

Codes:

(a) (i), (ii), (iii), (iv) (b) (i), (iii), (ii), (iv)

(c) (ii), (i), (iii), (iv) (d) (iii), (i), (iv), (ii)

33. Arrange the following States chronologically according to year of enactment of Library Legislation

(i) Tamil Nadu (1948) (ii) U.P. (2006)

(iii) Gujarat (2000) (iv) Mizoram (1994)

Codes:

(a) (iv), (iii), (i), (ii) (b) (ii), (iv), (iii), (i)

(c) (i), (iv), (iii), (ii) (d) (i), (ii), (iv), (iii)

34. Arrange the following chronologically according to their use in computers:

(i) Vacuum tube (ii) Microchip

(iii) Integrated circuits (iv) Transistors

Codes:

(a) (i), (iii), (ii), (iv) (b) (i), (ii), (iii), (iv)

(c) (i), (iv), (iii), (ii) (d) (ii), (iv), (iii), (i)

35. Arrange the following professional associations according to the year of their establishment:

(i) ILA (ii) IASLIC

(iii) ALA (iv) ASLIB

Codes:

(a) (i), (ii), (iii), (iv) **(b) (iii), (iv), (i), (ii)**

(c) (iv), (iii), (ii), (i) (d) (i), (iii), (ii), (iv)

36. Arrange the following according to chronological order:

(i) Universal Copyright convention (1952)

(ii) Berne Convention (1886)

(iii) Indian Copyright Act (1957)

(iv) WIPO Copyright Act (1996)

(a) (ii), (iv), (iii), (i) (b) (iii), (ii), (iv), (i)

(c) (i), (iii), (ii), (iv) **(d) (ii), (i), (iii), (iv)**

37. Arrange the structure of the Research report in correct order:

(i) Table of contents (ii) Appendices

(iii) Text (iv) Title page

Codes:

(a) (iii), (i), (iv), (ii) (b) (i), (ii), (iii), (iv)
(c) (ii), (iii), (iv), (i) **(d) (iv), (i), (iii), (ii)**

38. Arrange the following schemes of classification according to their year of publication:
(i) CC (1933) (ii) DDC (1876)
(iii) LC (1901) (iv) UDC (1895)

Codes:

(a) (ii), (i), (iii), (iv) **(b) (ii), (iv), (iii), (i)**
(c) (i), (ii), (iv), (iii) (d) (iv), (iii), (ii), (i)

39. Match the following:

List-I	**List-II**
(a) The Right to Information Act	(i) 2000
(b) Universal Declaration of Human Rights	(ii) 2005
(c) Information Technology Act (India)	(iii) 1948
(d) Digital Millennium Act	(iv) 1998

Codes:

	(a)	(b)	(c)	(d)
(a)	(i)	(ii)	(iii)	(iv)
(b)	**(ii)**	**(iii)**	**(i)**	**(iv)**
(c)	(iii)	(ii)	(iv)	(i)
(d)	(iv)	(iii)	(ii)	(i)

40. Match the following:

List-I	**List-II**
(a) Father of Scientific Management	(i) Henry Fayol
(b) Father of Administration	(ii) Elton Mayo
(c) Father of Human Relations School	(iii) F.Hertzberg
(d) Father of Corporate Strategy	(iv) F.W.Taylor

Codes:

	(a)	(b)	(c)	(d)
(a)	(iv)	(ii)	(i)	(iii)
(b)	**(iv)**	**(i)**	**(ii)**	**(iii)**
(c)	(iii)	(iv)	(ii)	(i)
(d)	(ii)	(iii)	(iv)	(i)

41. Match the following;

List-I	List-II
(a) C.A.Cutter	(i) Bibliographic classification
(b) H.E.Bliss	(ii) Expansive classification
(c) J.D.Brown	(iii) Universal classification
(d) Paul Otlet & Henry La Fontaine	(iv) Subject classification

Codes:

	(a)	(b)	(c)	(d)
(a)	**(ii)**	**(i)**	**(iv)**	**(iii)**
(b)	(ii)	(iii)	(iv)	(i)
(c)	(i)	(iii)	(iv)	(ii)
(d)	(iii)	(iv)	(ii)	(i)

42. Match the following:

List-I	List-II
(a) International Conference on cataloguing Principles	(i) 1969
(b) International Meeting of Cataloguing Experts	(ii) 1961
(c) International Symposium of Bibliographic Exchange Format	(iii) 1990
(d) First CCF Users meeting	(iv) 1978

Codes:

	(a)	(b)	(c)	(d)
(a)	**(ii)**	**(i)**	**(iv)**	**(iii)**
(b)	(iii)	(ii)	(iv)	(i)
(c)	(iv)	(iii)	(i)	(ii)
(d)	(iii)	(i)	(iv)	(ii)

43. Match the following:

List-I	List-II
(a) NASSDOC	(i) Defence Science
(b) DEVSIS	(ii) Social Sciences
(c) INIS	(iii) Development Science
(d) DESIDOC	(iv) Nuclear Science

Codes:

	(a)	(b)	(c)	(d)
(a)	(iv)	(ii)	(i)	(iii)
(b)	**(ii)**	**(iii)**	**(iv)**	**(i)**
(c)	(i)	(ii)	(iii)	(iv)
(d)	(iii)	(ii)	(i)	(iv)

44. Match the following:

List-I	List-II
(a) CLRI	(i) Hyderabad
(b) SENDOC	(ii) New Delhi
(c) NASSDOC	(iii)Mumbai
(d) BARC	(iv)Chennai

Codes:

	(a)	(b)	(c)	(d)
(a)	(ii)	(i)	(iv)	(iii)
(b)	(iv)	(iii)	(i)	(ii)
(c)	**(iv)**	**(i)**	**(ii)**	**(iii)**
(d)	(iii)	(i)	(iv)	(ii)

45. Match the following:

List-I	List-II
(a) Fumigation	(i) Acquisition
(b) Building library collection	(ii) Preservation
(c) Kardex	(iii)Reference service
(d) Information desk	(iv)Registration of Periodicals

Codes:

	(a)	(b)	(c)	(d)
(a)	(ii)	(iii)	(i)	(iv)
(b)	(ii)	(iii)	(iv)	(i)
(c)	(iii)	(ii)	(i)	(iv)
(d)	**(ii)**	**(i)**	**(iv)**	**(iii)**

COMPREHENSION TEST:

46. What is an invention?

(a) It is the idea that has the characteristics of application

(b) A theoretical idea regardless of application
(c) A discovery that does not lead to new technology
(d) A process bereft of use

47. An invention involves
(a) Collection & application of past data
(b) Simply an effort to explore past knowledge
(c) Redefining knowledge of the past
(d) Exploiting past knowledge and newly collected facts

48. Industrial development and competitive environment are possible when
(a) Invention follows innovation
(b) Invention leads to innovation
(c) Invention prevents innovation
(b) Invention has little practical use

49. Invention is carried out at present
(a) By an individual researcher with little originality and imagination
(b) By an individual researcher with high level imagination
(c) By a group of researchers with adequate originality and imagination
(d) By industrialists to achieve success in business

50. What is innovation?
(a) Innovation is a theoretical process
(b) Innovation conceals invention
(c) Innovation is a process of application of invention
(d) Innovation provides data for invention

December 2010

1. Linear model of communication in knowledge based on Aristotles' model of communication was proposed by
   (a) Juger Heberman
   (b) A.J.Wells
   (c) C.E.Shannon & W.Weaver
   (d) G.Gerbner
2. ISBN changed from 10 digits to 13 from
   (a) January, 2007 (b) January, 2008
   (c) January, 2006 (d) January, 2005
3. Library legislation refers to the development of
   (a) Academic Libraries (b) Special Libraries
   (c) Public Libraries (d) None of the above
4. IASLIC was founded in the year
   (a) 1955 (b) 1965
   (c) 1975 (d) 1985
5. Which bibliometric Law describes the frequency of publication by authors in a given field?
   (a) Lotka's Law (b) Zipf's Law
   (c) Bradford's Law (d) None of the above
6. Which one of the following protocols is used in transferring file over internet?
   (a) POP (b) FTP
   (c) SMTP **(d) TCP/IP**
7. Transistors were used in which generation of computers?
   (a) First generation **(b) Second generation**
   (c) Third generation (d) None of the above
8. UNIMARC was developed under the umbrella of
   (a) OCLC **(b) IFLA**
   (c) UNESCO (d) None of the above
9. How different nodes in a network are connected and how they communicate are determined?
   (a) By Network Connectivity

(b) By Network Topology
(c) By Network Compatibility
(d) None of the above

11. WorldCat is maintained by
(a) Library of Congress
(b) Online Computer Library Center
(c) American Library Association
(d) None of the above

12. Number of States in India which have enacted Public Library Legislation till date is
(a) Seven (b) Ten
(c) Thirteen **(d) Sixteen**

13. When a source referred to once in the footnote is referred to again and between them no other reference (i.e. citation) intervenes, then the footnote uses the abbreviation
(a) Ibid (b) Id
(c) Op.Cit. (d) None of the above

14. Indexing system in which the coordination of terms is done at the search stage was first introduced by
(a) S.R.Ranganathan (b) Derek Austin
(c) Mortimer Taube (d) H.P.Luhn

15. Index Medicus is brought out as printed publication
(a) Quarterly **(b) Monthly**
(c) Weekly (d) Has ceased publication

16. Which publication was not authored by S.R.Ranganathan?
(a) Prolegomena to library classification
(b) Reference Service
(c) Ramanujan: The man and the Mathematician
(d) Living with Books

17. JSTOR is an online system for archiving and accessing academic journals. It is located in
(a) Germany **(b) UK**
(c) USA (d) Budapest

18. 260 tag in MARC format marks
    (a) The edition
    (b) The publication information
    (c) The physical description
    (d) A topical subject heading
19. Mean, Median and Mode are
    (a) Measure of Central Tendency
    (b) Measure of Deviation
    (c) Measure of Information System
    (d) Measure of Sampling
20. 'Five Laws of Library Science' was first published in
    (a) 1925 (b) 1930
    (c) 1931 (d) 1933
21. **Assertion (A):** ISBDs were devised by UNESCO
    Reason (R): They are the standards for all types of bibliographic activities.
    (a) (A) is false but (R) is true
    (b) (A) is true but (R) is false
    (c) Both (A) and (R) are true
    (d) Both (a) and (R) are false.
22. **Assertion (A):** Web OPAC is a computerised library catalogue available to the patrons online.
    Reason (R): It can be searched by the users within the four walls of the library only.
    (a) (A) is true but (R) is false
    (b) (A) is false but (R) is true
    (c) Both (A) and (R) are true
    (d) Both (A) and (R) are false.
23. **Assertion (A):** A sample is the representation of a whole.
    Reason (R): The sample is subjected to observation and analysis.
    (a) (A) is false but (R) is true
    (b) (A) is true but (R) is false
    (c) Both (A) and (R) are true
    (d) Both (A) and (R) are false

24. **Assertion (A):** Electronic access to information is becoming easy day by day.

    Reason (R): The printed materials pouring out of the world presses do not show any decline.

    (a) Both (A) and (R) are true but (R) is not a correct explanation of (A).

    (b) (A) is true but (R) is false.

    (c) (A) is false but (R) is true.

    (d) Both (A) and (R) are false.

25. **Assertion (A):** Use of microfilming is becoming obsolete day by day.

    Reason (R): ICT has developed digital technologies, which are quick, cheap and easy to handle.

    (a) Both (A) and (R) are true but (R) is not a correct explanation.

    (b) Both (A) and (R) are false

    (c) (A) is true but (R) is false

    (d) Both (A) and (R) are true and (R) is the correct explanation of (A).

26. **Assertion (A):** Libraries are changing in the wake of emerging ICT environment.

    Reason (R): Libraries are adopting new competencies to operate services in the environment of information super highways.

    (a) Both (A) and (R) are true

    (b) (A) is true but (R) is false

    (c) (A) is false but (R) is true

    (d) Both (A) and (R) are false

27. **Assertion (A):** In fifth law, the word used in 'organism' not 'organisation'.

    Reason (R): Libraries grow in collection size, human resources, physical facilities and services from time to time.

(a) Both (A) and (R) are true and (R) is the correct explanation of (A)

(b) Both (A) and (R) are true but (R) is not the correct explanation of (A).

(c) (A) is true but (R) is false.

(d) (A) is false but (R) is true.

28. **Assertion (A):** Primary source is one in which information is original.

Reason (R): Secondary sources repack the original information.

(a) Both (A) and (R) are true.

(b) (A) is true but (R) is false.

(c) (A) is false but (R) is true.

(d) Both (A) and (R) are false.

29. **Assertion (A):** Loose Assemblage is the process of linking together different classes.

Reason (R): This mode was formerly known as subject bundle.

(a) (A) is false but (R) is true

(b) (A) is true but (R) is false

(c) Both (A) and (R) are true

(d) Both (A) and (R) are false.

30. **Assertion (A):** Provision of services outside the library regular service centre or outlet is essential to reach more and more patrons.

Reason (R): Library extension services help libraries to cover larger population of patrons.

(a) (A) is true but (R) is true.

(b) (A) is false but (R) is true.

(c) Both (A) and (R) are true.

(d) Both (A) and (R) are false.

31. Arrange the following in chronological sequence:

(i) Digital Millennium Copyright Act

(ii) Right to Information Act (India)

(iii) Information Technology Act (India)

(iv) Indian Copyright Act

Codes:

(a) (iv), (i), (iii), (ii) (b) (iv), (ii), (iii), (i)

(c) (i), (iv), (ii), (iii) (d) (ii), (iii), (i), (iv)

32. Arrange the following States according to the year of enactment of library legislation:

(i) Pondicherry (ii) Orissa

(iii) Rajasthan (iv) Karnataka

Codes:

(a) (iv), (i), (iii), (ii) **(b) (iv), (ii), (iii), (i)**

(c) (iv), (iii), (i), (ii) (d) (i), (iii), (ii), (iv)

33. Arrange the following softwares according to their development:

(i) E-Print (ii) DSpace

(iii) Greenstone (iv) Koha

Codes:

(a) (iv), (iii), (ii), (i) (b) (iii), (ii), (i), (iv)

(c) (i), (ii), (iii), (iv) (d) (ii), (iii), (iv), (i)

34. Arrange the following steps in research in the sequence of their occurrence:

(i) Report writing (ii) Research design

(iii) Collection of data (iv) Analysis of data

Codes:

(a) (iii), (iv), (ii), (i) (b) (i), (iii), (iv), (ii)

(c) (ii), (iii), (iv), (i) (d) (iv), (ii), (iii), (i)

35. Arrange the following chronologically according to their year of Birth:

(i) S.R.Ranganathan (1892-1972)

(ii) Melvil Dewey

(iii) C.A.Cutter (1837-1903)

(iv) B.S.Kesavan

Codes:

(a) (ii), (i), (iv), (iii) (b) (i), (iii), (iv), (ii)

(c) (iii), (ii), (i), (iv) (d) (iv), (i), (ii), (iii)

36. Arrange the following chronologically according to their development:

(i) Punched Card

(ii) Floppy Disc (1.44 MB)

(iii) Magnetic Disc (20-1000 MB)

(iv) Optical Disc (700 MB-4.7 GB)

Codes:

(a) (ii), (iii), (i), (iv)
(b) (i), (iii), (ii), (iv)
(c) (i), (ii), (iii), (iv)
(d) (iv), (i), (ii), (iii)

37. Arrange the following according to their development:

(i) CCC (1934)
(ii) ISBD (1969)
(iii) CCF (1978)
(iv) MARCII (1968)

Codes:

(a) (i), (iv), (ii), (iii)
(b) (i), (ii), (iv), (iii)
(c) (i), (iv), (iii), (ii)
(d) (iv), (ii), (iii), (i)

38. The spiral of scientific method involves the following steps in correct sequence:

(i) Zenith
(ii) Ascendant
(iii) Nadir
(iv) Descendant

Codes:

(a) (i), (iii), (ii), (iv)
(b) (ii), (iii), (i), (iv)
(c) (iii), (ii), (i), (iv)
(d) (i), (iv), (iii), (ii)

39. Match the following:

List-I	**List-II**
(a) AACR-I	(i) 1978
(b) AACR-2	(ii) 1967
(c) ALA Code	(iii) 1934
(d) CCC	(iv) 1949

Codes:

	(a)	(b)	(c)	(d)
(a)	(iv)	(ii)	(iii)	(i)
(b)	(ii)	(i)	(iii)	(iv)
(c)	(i)	(iii)	(iv)	(ii)
(d)	**(ii)**	**(i)**	**(iv)**	**(iii)**

40. Match the following:

List-I	**List-II**
(a) Books in print	(i) Bibliography of periodicals
(b) Ulrich International Periodical Directory	(ii) Trade Bibliography
(c) World of Learning	(iii) Biographical source
(d) Who's Who in India	(iv) Directory

Codes:

	(a)	(b)	(c)	(d)
(a)	**(ii)**	**(i)**	**(iv)**	**(iii)**
(b)	(i)	(ii)	(iii)	(iv)
(c)	(iii)	(i)	(iv)	(ii)
(d)	(ii)	(i)	(iv)	(iii)

41. Match the following:

List-I	**List-II**
(a) Henry Fayol	(i) Hierarchy Needs
(b) F.W.Taylor	(ii) Theory X and Theory Y
(c) Abraham Maslow	(iii)Classical Theory
(d) Douglas McGregor	(iv) Scientific Manmagemn

Codes:

	(a)	(b)	(c)	(d)
(a)	**(iii)**	**(iv)**	**(i)**	**(ii)**
(b)	(i)	(ii)	(iii)	(iv)
(c)	(iv)	(iii)	(ii)	(i)
(d)	(i)	(iv)	(iii)	(ii)

42. Match the following:

List-I	**List-II**
(a) E.J.Coates	(i) KWIC
(b) H.P.Luhn	(ii) Things, Property, material, Action
(c) Derek Austin	(iii) Concrete and process
(d) J.Kaiser	(iv) PRECIS

Codes:

	(a)	(b)	(c)	(d)
(a)	(i)	(ii)	(iii)	(iv)
(b)	**(ii)**	**(i)**	**(iv)**	**(iii)**
(c)	(iii)	(ii)	(i)	(iv)
(d)	(iv)	(i)	(ii)	(iii)

43. Match the following:

List-I	**List-II**
(a) NTC	(i) UK
(b) ITC	(ii) India
(c) BLDSC	(iii) Netherlands
(d) NISCAIR	(iv) USA

Codes:

	(a)	(b)	(c)	(d)
(a)	**(iv)**	**(iii)**	**(i)**	**(ii)**
(b)	(ii)	(i)	(iv)	(iii)
(c)	(i)	(iii)	(ii)	(iv)
(d)	(i)	(ii)	(iii)	(iv)

44. Match the following:

List-I **(Subjects)**	**List-II** **(Modes of Formation)**
(a) India	(i) Agglomeration
(b) Agriculture of Wheat	(ii) Lamination
(c) Biochemistry	(iii)Fusion
(d) Biological Sciences	(iv) Denudation

Codes:

	(a)	(b)	(c)	(d)
(a)	**(iv)**	**(ii)**	**(iii)**	**(i)**
(b)	(i)	(iii)	(ii)	(iv)
(c)	(iv)	(iii)	(i)	(ii)
(d)	(ii)	(iv)	(iii)	(i)

45. Match the following:

List-I	**List-II**
(a) Elements of Library Classification	(i) D.J.De Solla Price

(b) Little Science big Science	(ii) S.R.Ranganathan
(c) Documentation	(iii) D.J.Fosket
(d) Subject Approach to Information	(iv) S.C.Bradford

Codes:

	(a)	(b)	(c)	(d)
(a)	**(ii)**	**(i)**	**(iv)**	**(iii)**
(b)	(iii)	(ii)	(i)	(iv)
(c)	(iv)	(ii)	(iii)	(i)
(d)	(i)	(ii)	(iii)	(iv)

COMPREHENSION TEST:

46. What are DOIs?
    (a) DOIs are numbers which identify object in traditional environment
    (b) DOIs are identifiers consisting consisting of alphanumeric character strings for printed materials
    (c) DOIs are alphanumeric character strings for electronic serials
    (d) DOIs are alphanumeric character strings for electronic sources of information available on-line.

47. What are the materials covered by DOIs?
    (a) DOIs cover books and journals
    (b) DOIs cover texts, images, audio visual materials in digital form
    (c) DOIs cover electronically available S & T information
    (d) DOis cover digital format in US and Europe only.

48. Do DOIs play any role in grouping of information sources?
    (a) DOIs constitute the e-classification scheme to group sources of information
    (b) DOIs are not class numbers as such and have nothing to do with arrangement

(c) DOIs play the dual role of identifying and grouping

(d) DOIs are only like traditional class numbers in e-form.

49. What is the major purpose of DOIs system?

(a) To organise e-resources on the Net

(b) To manage intellectual property

(c) To provide bibliographic description of digitized resources

(d) To control free access to e-resources.

50. How does DOI system operate?

(a) Routes inquiries to designated Document Supply Libraries

(b) Routes inquires to up to date

(c) Routes inquiries to national e-resources depositories

(d) Routes inquiries to relevant sites on the Net.

SOME SHORT QUESTIONS AND ANSWERS IN DIFFERENT STYLE

1. Standard size of catalogue card first suggested by **C.A.Cutter**
2. "Econometrics"-which mode of subject formation? Fusion
3. Concept of FRBR by **IFLA Cataloguing Section's Working Group on FRBR,** *chaired by* Patrick LeBoeuf.
4. Which research method is useful to count active life of periodicals? **Bibliometric Research Method (Half Life Theory)**
5. Formula of Recall ratio—**No. of Relevant Term Retrieved/Total No. of Indexing Terms Searched**
6. Idea of citation indexing 1st defined by **Eugene Garfield.**
7. INIS collaborated with **BARC** in India.
8. Arrange in chronological order—AACR2 (4), CCC (2),AA code (1), ALA code (3)
9. Library 2.0 is coined by **Michael Casey.**
10. WWW is coined by **Timothy John Berners Lee** (1980).
11. Unified Resource Identifier (URI), HTTP, HTML, and RDF (Notation3) are coined by **Timothy John Berners Lee.**
12. Information Superhighway is coined by **Nam June Paik**.
14. Web 2.0 is coined by **Dale Dougherty** and **Tim O'Reilly** in O'Reilly Media Inc. in 2004.
15. Wiki is coined by **Howard G. Cunningham** in 1995.
16. Technologies associated with Web 2.0 are **RSS, RIA, Wiki, folksonomy, Tagging, Mashup**
17. RSS was first invented by **Netscape**.
18. Folksonomy is coined by **Thomas Vander Wal.**
19. Weblog is coined by **John Barger** in 1997.
20. Blog is coined by **Peter Merholz** in 1999.
21. Modern Blog is evolved from **Personal Diary.**
22. Internet services through cables – **WAP, WLAN**.
23. Wireless Internet services – **WIFI, GPRS**.
24. Channels of Open Access Publishing: **Open Access**

Journals and Open Access Archives or Repositories.

25. Introduction of Open Access concept: **1893**.
26. First free scientific online eprint archive – arXiv.org (1991) by **Paul Ginsparg**.
27. One successful open access journals in 1990s – **Journal of Medical Internet Research.**
28. One Open Access Publisher – **Public Library of Science** (2001).
29. Open Access Declarations – Budapest OAI (2002), Bethesda Statement on OA Publishing (2003), Berlin Declaration on OA to Knowledge in the Science and Humanities (Oct 2003)
30. Open Access Journal Publishing – **EUCLID and ArXiv** (Cornell University), **JSTOR** (Princeton and Maryland Universities), **Highware and LOCKSS** (Stanford University).
31. Ning was co-founded by **Mark Andreessen** and **Gina Biomchini** in 2005.
32. Facebook was launched by **Mark Zuckerberg** (Harvard Univ) in February 2004.
33. **First Law –**

    (a) Moderate Library (b) Library Staff
    (c) Library Building (d) Location of a Library
    (e) Library Hours (f) Book Selection
    (g) Shelf Arrangement (h) Reference Service
    (i) Maintenance
34. **Second Law –**

    (a) Library Legislation (b) Book Selection
    (c) Shelf Arrangement (d) Cataloguing
    (e) Maintenance (f) Reference Service
    (g) Resource Sharing (h) Open Access
    (i) Responsibility of the Users
35. **Third Law –**

    (a) Book Selection (b)Shelf Arrangement
    (c) Cataloguing (d) Reference Service
    (e) Accessibility (f) Extension Service

36. **Fourth Law –**
    (a) Shelf Arrangement (b) Cataloguing
    (c) Centralized Cataloguing and Classification
    (d) Library Services
    (e) Qualifications of a Reference Librarian
    (f) Accessibility
    (g) Signage System
    (h) Library Guide
    (i) Location of a Library
    (j) Special Sequences of Books
    (k) Library Publicity
    (l) Information Technology
    (m) Management of Libraries
    (n) Saving Time of the Staff
37. **Fifth Law –**
    (a) Implications of Growth
    (b) Choice of Classification Scheme
    (c) Shelf Arrangement
    (d) Choice of Catalogue Code
    (e) Physical Form of a catalogue
    (f) Reference Service
    (g) User Education
    (h) Library orientation
    (i) Staff
    (j) Restraint
38. **1st generation computer** – valves & tubes. **2nd generation computer** – transistor. **3rd generation computer** – very large integrated circuit (very large scale integrated circuit). **4th generation computer** – small integrated circuit (small scale integrated circuit)
39. UAP was launched by **Maurice B.Line.**
40. Brown Charging System – Ms. Nine E.Brown
41. Newark Charging System – **John Cotton Dana** (1900)
42. Canon of Cataloguing – **1937**
43. Canon of Recall Value – **1969**

44. **Library Legislation (World Wide)**

New York – 1835 (USA)
New Hempshire – 1849 (USA)
England & Wales – 1850
Canada, Connecticut – 1867
Japan – 1899
Czechoslovakia – 1910
Sweden – 1912
Denmark & USSR – 1920
Kolhapur – 1945 and Hyderabad - 1955 (India) non functional

45. **Library Legislation in India (Statewise)**

Tamil Nadu – 1948
Andhra Pradesh – 1960
Maharashtra – 1967
West Bengal – 1979
Manipur – 1988
Kerala – 1989
Haryana – 1989
Mizoram – 1993
Goa – 1994
Gujarat – 2000
Orissa – 2001
Rajasthan – 2005
Uttarakhand – 2005
U.P. – 2006
Pondicherry – 2008
Bihar – 2008

46. **Parts of a Book**

1. Preliminaries
   - (i) Book jacket
   - (ii) Cover page
   - (iii) Spine
   - (iv) Fly leaves
   - (v) Half-title page (Bastard title)

(vi) Title page
(vii) Frontispiece
(viii) Verso of the title page
(ix) Dedication
(x) Announcement
(xi) The Imprimature or License of Publication
(xii) The Forward
(xiii) Acknowledegements
(xiv) List of Abbreviations
(xv) Errata or Corrigenda
(xvi) Preface
(xvii) Table of contents
(xviii) List of Illustration
(xix) Introduction

2. Text
3. Subsidiaries/End matter

(xx) Appendices
(xxi) Bibliography
(xxii) Index
(xxiii) Exceptions
(xxiv) Notes
(xxv) Colophon
(xxvi) Finis
(xxvii)Plates and Maps

47. **Parts of the Journal/Periodical**

1 Name
2 Publishers
3 Place
4 Frequency
5 Suppliers/Source
6 Subscription amount
7 Year
8 Vol. No.
9 Issue no., Date
10 Binding record

11 ISSN
12 Procurement procedure
13 Supplement/Newsletter
14 Table of contents
15 Back of the cover page
16 List from Deptt.
17 Contributor's note
18 Forthcoming issue
19 Statement about honourship
20 Editorial Board/Forum
21 Call for papers
22 Instruction for authors
23 Lack issue reminder
24 Claim for non-receipt issue
25 Introduction
26 Errata
27 Selected list published journals

48. Op.cit. – **opere citato** (in the work cited, but different pages)
49. i.e. – **id est**
50. e.g. – **example gratia**
51. **DDC DETAILS:**

Edition	Year of Publication	Page No.	Copies	Editor(s)
1	1876 (1 Vol.)	42	1000	M.Dewey
2	1885 (1 Vol.)	314	500	M.Dewey & W.S.Biscoe
3	1888 (1 Vol.)	416	500	M.Dewey & W.S.Biscoe
4	1891 (1 Vol.)	466	1000	May Seymour
5	1894 (1 Vol.)	467	2000	May Seymour
6	1899 (1 Vol.)	511	7600	May Seymour
7	1911 (1 Vol.)	792	2000	May Seymour
8	1913 (1 Vol.)	850	2000	May Seymour
9	1915 (1 Vol.)	856	3000	May Seymour
10	1919 (1 Vol.)	940	4000	May Seymour
11	1922 (1 Vol.)	988	5000	Dorkas Fellows
12	1927 (1 Vol.)	1243	9340	Dorkas Fellows
13	1932 (1 Vol.)	1647	9750	D.Fellows & M.W. Getchell

14	1942 (1 Vol.)	1927	15632	Constantin Mazney & M.W.Ge
15	1951 (1 Vol.)	716	11200	Milton J. Ferguson
15R	1952 (1Vol.)	927	11045	Geoffrey Dewey
16	1958 (2Vols.)	2439	31011	Benjamin Custer & D. Heykin
17	1965 (2Vols.)	2153	38677	Benjamin Custer & D. Heykin
17R	1967 (2 Vols.)	2480		Benjamin A. Custer
18	1971 (3Vols.)	2718		Benjamin A. Custer
19	1979 (3 Vols.)	3385		Benjamin A. Custer
20	1990 (4 Vols.)	3388		John P. Comaromi
21	1996 (4 Vols.)	+ DDC for Windows		John S. Mitchell et.al.
22	2003 (4 Vols.)	4058+ DDC for Windows		John S. Mitchell, Juliannw Beall, Giles Martin, Winton E. Matthews, Gregory R. New

52. Classification Theory

Level	*Name of Normative Principles*
Basic process of thinking	Basic Laws
Library Science	Fundamental Laws
Classification	Canon
Helpful sequence in array	Principles
Work of Classifying	Postulates and principles for facet sequence

BASIC LAWS

(i) Law of Interpretation (ii) Law of Impartiality
(iii) Law of Symmetry (iv) Law of Parsimony
(v) Law of Local Variation (vi) Law of Osmosis.

53. **What is MESH?** MESH is a Thesaurus. [The content of data elements in MARC records is defined by standards outside the formats such as AACR2, Library of Congress Subject Headings, and Medical Subject Headings (MeSH)].

58. **Brief profile on LIS Education.**

- First library school in the world – 1887 (Columbia University, USA by Melvil Dewey)
- First library school in India – 1911 (by W.A.Borden

disciple of M.Dewey at Baroda)

- First Univ. level Library Science course – 1915 (Panjab University presently in Lahore, Pakistan)
- Training course in Andhra Desha Library Association – 1920 (at Vijawada)
- Certificate course in Lib.Sc. -1929 (by Madras Library Association)
- Certificate course in Lib.Sc. -1935 (by Bengal Library Association at Banasberia)
- Post Graduate course – 1936 (by Univ. of Madras)
- Post Graduate diploma – 1942 (by Banaras Hindu University)
- Post Graduate course – 1948 (by Delhi Univ.) <later named as B.Lib.Sc.
- B.Lib.Sc. course – 1957 (by Aligarh Muslim University)
- B.Lib.Sc. – 1960 (by Univ. of Madras)
- DRTC – 1962 (ADIS), INSDOC – 1964 (AIS), IGNOU – 1989 (BLIS), 1996 (MLIS)
- 90 universities offered – CLIS to Ph.D.
- 5 Open Universities offered – BLIS & MLIS
- 21 universities offered regular course as well as correspondence course

55. **Library Management Software developer**

Alice for Windows – Softlink International (Australia); Basisplus & Techlibplus – Information Dimensions, Inc., USA & NIC (India); VirtualLS – VTLS Inc., Virginia (USA); LAMP – Netherlands Library Association, Pakistan Library Association and UNESCO (based on CDS/ISIS version 3.07); NG-TLMS.NET – Trance Group, Germany <Total Library Management System>; Autolib – Autolib Software, Chennai; Nexlib – NexEvolve Logic Solutions Pvt. Ltd.; SLIM – Algorithms Pvt. Ltd., Pune <Software for Lib. Inf. Management>